SARguide for a better sex life

A self-help program for personal sexual enrichment/education designed by The National Sex Forum

Copyright © 1975 by The National Sex Forum

Illustrations pages 33-45 © 1974 by Leona Walden

All reproductions of art work courtesy International Museum of Erotic Art
© Drs. Phyllis and Eberhard Kronhausen for The National Sex Forum

L.C. Number 75-7218
ISBN 0-913566-01-2

ACKNOWLEDGEMENTS

Thanks to all the people who have made important contributions to the development of the SAR program presented in this book, especially to: Mary Briggs, Joani Blank, Lonnie Barbach, Betty Dodson, Carol Olsen, Lonnie Myers, Pepper Schwartz, Rick Chilgren, Ted Cole, Peter Endes, Bernie Zilbergeld, Tom Mooney, Herb Vandervoort, Bill and Ella Marie Hunt.

Thanks to Jessie Potter and Don Shaw for the use of their *Sex Attitude and Experience Survey*, reprinted with many changes in the Sexual Experience Survey portion of the SARguide.

Thanks to Len Laskow for his contribution to the development of the sexological exam.

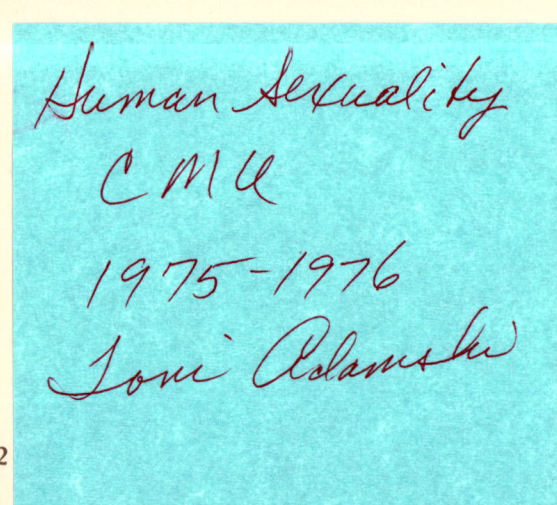

CONTENTS

Acknowledgments 2

Preface 5

How to Use this SARguide 6

Calendar of At Home Exercises 8

Curriculum Outline—
Weekly Schedule for Class Discussion 10

Weekly Schedule of Video Cassettes 11

SECTION A
Introduction 13
What it Takes to Make it Work 16
Situational Assessment 17
Sexual Experience Survey 17
Contract 30
Use of Journal 31
At Home Exercises—To Do Before First Group
Session 32

SECTION B
Informational Reading
Anatomy and Physiology of the Sexual
Response Cycle 49
Fantasy 56
Masturbation 59
Sensate Focus 62
Video
"Unfolding"
"Margo"
"Shirley"
"Feeling Good"
At Home Exercises 64

SECTION C
Informational Reading
Male Sexuality 72
Male Homosexuality 74
Desensitization 77
Female Sexuality 81
Lesbianism 88
Bisexuality 91
Celibacy 94
Video
"Gay View/Male"
"Vir Amat"
"Titles Available"
"Rich and Judy"
"Free"
"Sun Brushed"
"Fullness"
"Joy in Her Pleasure"
"Closing the Circle"
At Home Exercises 96

SECTION D
Informational Reading
Massage 106
Video
"In Winter Light"
"Gay View/Female"
"Sexological Exam"
"A Ripple in Time"
"Both/And"
At Home Exercises 109

SECTION E
Informational Reading
Disability 116
Video
"Touching"
"The Squeeze Technique"
"Erogenists"
"Give to Get"
How to Continue This Course 118
At Home Exercises for Enrichment 119

Appendix
Lubricants 124
Genital Hygiene 124
Sexual Concerns 125
Additional Resource Information 127

About the Authors 128

PREFACE

What Is This Book?

This SARguide is a workbook, an adjunct to the National Sex Forum's Personal Sexual Enrichment/Education program. PSE/E is a low-cost self-help program based on the SAR Process (Sexual Attitude Restructuring) developed by the Forum. PSE/E uses video cassette tapes in conjunction with a skilled counselor to help persons change and expand sexual attitudes and actions. It is a simple step-by-step process to open to you all the possibilities of sexuality; to enhance your senses; to give you joy, pleasure and freedom to feel.

If you are not in an area where the PSE/E program is available you can learn much about your sexuality and the sexuality of others by reading this book, by doing the homework assignments and by filling out the sex history questionnaire.

We wish you all a better, happier and more fulfilling sex life.

Staff of the National Sex Forum

Toni Ayres
Phyllis Lyon
Ted McIlvenna
Frank Myers
Margo Rila
Maggi Rubenstein
Carolyn Smith
Laird Sutton

February, 1975

HOW TO USE THIS SARGUIDE

General information

The SARguide for a better sex life is a guide to a step by step educational process. As such, persons expecting to get maximum benefits from the program should not attempt to do everything in this guide all at once. The SARguide includes at home and in class exercises which involve several different aspects of ourselves; our breathing, our body movements, all of our senses, our emotions, our attitudes towards ourselves and others, our communication with partners, our sexual identity.

There is also much factual information about sexuality. This combination of information and experience has enabled many women and men to develop a solid basis for making decisions regarding their sexuality and to have a more comfortable feeling about their total sexual selves. There are no prohibitions of intercourse necessary in this program. Participants are encouraged to continue doing whatever they usually feel comfortable doing. You make your contract for change only with yourself.

Taking the course

You can take this course by yourself or come with a sexual partner or friend. There are at home exercises to be done for yourself and with a partner. If you currently do not have a particular sexual partner then concentrate on the exercises for yourself.

Finding your way through this guide

- The edges of the SARguide pages are keyed to sections A through E so you can find the sections easily.
- The Table of Contents gives you the page numbers and groupings of topics for each step of the course.
- The Curriculum Outline (page 10) and the List of Video Sequences (page 11) will help you integrate the class sessions, informational readings, and video materials directly to the at home exercises.
- The Program Calendar of at home exercises (pages 8 and 9) will serve as your key to what to do next. A list of the appropriate at home exercises for each week is also repeated in each section.

Information

The informational reading units are designed to be read *before* each weekly discussion and video section. A list of what to read next is provided at the end of each section.

Video

The video descriptions in each section are simply helpful hints on what to look for when you see the video in class.

Exercises

The exercises in the guide are designed in sequence for maximum success in learning on your own at *your* own pace. You may decide a particular exercise is not appropriate to you at the time given. If so, don't do it. Remember it, make a notation in the calendar or list of exercises in each section, and do it when it will be of use to you.

Timing

How you pace yourself in this Personal Sexual Enrichment/Education program is important. If you go too fast you will miss some of the potential of the experience. On the other hand, if you go too slow you will lose the rewarding feelings that go with learning to grow. We encourage you to stay in the present, to be here now, so that you can benefit from the reinforced learning. It's up to you to choose for yourself how fast you move and how many things you want to change, if any. You can follow the calendar week by week. Several of the exercises are designed to be repeated—they don't take much time and are important to keep doing.

Journal

An important part of this program is the journal you keep. Don't neglect this. If you ever feel you have "failed" an at home exercise, write down in your journal what you learned from the experience. **There are no failures or grades in this program, only learning experiences.**

CALENDAR OF AT HOME EXERCISES

	SECTION A (After Situational Survey)	**SECTION B** (Week # 1)
GETTING IN TOUCH WITH SELF	1. Take Time & Space for Self 2. Breathing Exercises a-h 3. Sensory Awareness Exercises a-d 4. Kegels 5. Body Imagery 6. Journal Entries	1. Look at Two Types of Erotic Art 2. Imagine That: 3. Talk to Body 4. Genital Exam 5. Whole Body Masturbation 6. Masturbation with Teasing, Smelling, Tasting
GETTING IN TOUCH WITH PARTNER OR FRIEND	1. Breathing Exercise i (Spoon Breathing)	1. Talking and Listening 2. Masturbation Experience
REPEAT EXERCISES		1. Journal 2. Repeat Breathing Exercises a, c, d, i 3. Repeat Sensory Awareness Exercises a, b 4. Repeat Kegels

READ/REACH AHEAD FOR THE NEXT WEEK	1. How to Use this Guide
	2. Information Sections
	  a. Anatomy & Physiology
	  b. Fantasy
	  c. Masturbation
	  d. Sensate Focus
		1. Male Sexuality
		2. Male Homosexuality
		3. Desensitization
		4. Resensitization
		5. Female Sexuality
		6. Lesbianism
		7. Bisexuality
		8. Celibacy

SECTION C
(Week #2)

1. Masturbate in a New Way
2. Light Stroking
3. Incorporate Pelvic Breathing into Masturbation
4. Yes-&-No
5. Productive/Non-Productive Hour
6. Sex Words

1. Three Things to Change
2. Intercourse in New Position
3. Intercourse with Additional Stimulation

1. Journal
2. Breathing Exercises a, i
3. Sensory Awareness a, b
4. Kegels

1. Massage
2. Reread Female Sexuality, Bisexuality, & Lesbianism

SECTION D
(Week #3)

1. Masturbate with Something in Vagina or around Penis
2. Experience Awareness
3. Secret Intent
4. Get Something Sexy

1. Home Sexological
2. Informational Massage
3. Sharing Masturbation

1. Journal
2. Breathing Exercises a, i
3. Repeat Incorporating Breathing into Masturbation
4. Sensory Awareness a, b
5. Repeat Yes-&-No
6. Kegels

1. Disability
2. Enrichment

SECTION E
(Week #4)

1. Masturbation with Sounds
2. Fantasy Enrichment

1. Oral Sex

Go back and find the time to do exercises you liked.
Focus on exercises that will help you grow.
—Kegels
   Yes-&-No

Special Concerns (See Appendix)

CURRICULUM OUTLINE

WEEKLY SCHEDULE FOR CLASS DISCUSSION

	Class Session		Page
Anatomy & Physiology of the Sexual Response Cycle	I	Section B	49
Fantasy			56
Masturbation			59
Sensate Focus			62
Male Sexuality	II	Section C	72
Male Homosexuality			74
Desensitization			77
Female Sexuality			81
Lesbianism			88
Bisexuality			91
Celibacy			94
Massage	III	Section D	106
Disability	IV	Section E	116
How to Continue			118
Enrichment			119

WEEKLY SCHEDULE OF VIDEO CASSETTES

	Class Session		Page
Unfolding	I	Section B	63
Margo			
Shirley			
Feeling Good			
A Gay View / Male	II	Section C	94
Vir Amat			
Titles Available			
Rich and Judy			
Free			
Sun Brushed			
Fullness			
Joy in Her Pleasure			
Closing the Circle			
In Winter Light	III	Section D	108
A Gay View / Female			
Sexological Exam			
A Ripple in Time			
Both/And			
Touching	IV	Section E	117
Squeeze Technique			
The Erogenists			
Give to Get			

INTRODUCTION

The National Sex Forum was created because of the realization that almost everyone wants to have a better sex life; that persons doing counseling in the sexual area often do not know much about human sexuality; that most sex problems, difficulties and disappointments are a result of lack of information and a faulty attitude/value structure.

Born officially in October, 1968, the Forum was a service of San Francisco's Methodist-related Glide Foundation until January, 1973, when it became a service of Genesis Church and Ecumenical Center Trust, also in San Francisco.

The Forum developed the SAR Process (Sexual Attitude Restructuring), one of the most revolutionary methods ever designed for educating adults about what people do sexually and how they feel about it. This process is now being used by many medical schools and individuals throughout the world.

It all began in 1964, really, when Ted McIlvenna, a Methodist minister, came to The Glide Foundation to work with young people. He became acutely aware that among youth were many homosexual women and men very much alienated from the church. As he began to work with the Gay community he saw how much damage was done to homosexuals when they sought help from clergy, physicians and others and were rejected because of the bias and personal hang-ups of the counselors.

Realizing that you can't understand homosexuality without understanding human sexuality, McIlvenna and his staff began experimenting with a methodology which would help professional persons grasp a broader view of human sexuality. The answer seemed to lie in the use of sexually explicit films and slides. This format, much refined from the 1968 beginnings, is the basis today of the Forum's many training courses and of the program of Personal Sexual Enrichment/Education (PSE/E) to which this SARguide is an adjunct.

From the beginning the SAR Process has been geared to giving information, not to making judgments. The Forum feels that everyone has a right to a good sex life in whatever form she or he desires. Our job and our field of expertise is to present the facts about human sexuality. Your job and your field of expertise is to integrate these facts into your lifestyle and your value system.

Over the years more than 30,000 persons have taken the SAR process courses either through the National Sex Forum or through other groups using the process. Roughly half of these persons have been counselors, doctors, social workers or others in the "helping" professions. Statistics indicate that 96 percent find SAR very helpful both personally and professionally, 3 percent are not sure, and 1 percent find it of no value. The data obtained from these participants helped the Forum refine its methodology, proved that the process works, and started us on the road to the development of the Personal Sexual Enrichment/Education program.

The SAR process focuses on the following:

1. Endorsement (it is all right to be sexual, to know all there is to know about human sexuality).
2. Information giving (the history of sex research; what we know about human sexuality).
3. Information giving about our bodies (how we respond sexually).
4. Masturbation (the way most men and many women make their first commitment to sexuality).
5. Homosexuality in the female and the male (and bisexuality, an emerging sexual lifestyle).
6. Desensitization and resensitization (banishing sexual myths and replacing them with facts).
7. Female and male sexuality.

8. Sexual enrichment (how to have a better sex life).
9. Special problems (medical, religious, cultural, etc.).
10. Sexual therapy (impotence, premature ejaculation, pre-orgasmic women, physically or emotionally disabled persons, etc.).
11. Cultural expression (art, film, dance, music).

Because we wanted to use films and slides to illustrate the above areas we found it necessary to begin making our own films. Now there are some forty titles available from the Forum showing various aspects of human sexuality and sexual therapy techniques. These films, plus slides and tapes, are now being used throughout the world by agencies and individuals working in the fields of sex education, sex therapy and sex counseling.

For a long time we have been aware that persons attending the Forum's basic introductory course have in a great measure solved a lot of their sexual problems. This has also been observed by others in the sex field. Our conclusion is that most so-called sexual dysfunction results from lack of knowledge. Where there is no physical problem involved most persons find that they can change their patterns simply through a change in attitude and actions whether or not they have had difficulty in achieving orgasm, controlling premature ejaculation or maintaining potency.

It was the above knowledge plus the desire to give everyone a chance to have a better sex life that led us to design the low-cost, self-help, educational video cassette program called Personal Sexual Enrichment/Education. The program is not designed to solve all relationship problems. We do feel, however, that if a relationship is on rocky grounds it is helpful for the partners to get some factual information about their sexuality. They can then assess their relationship from a basis of knowledge and decide whether they also need individual counseling or couple counseling.

The work of the National Sex Forum is a logical progression in the history of the field of sex education in the United States. It is generally conceded that modern sex education began in the 1930s when Dr. Alfred Kinsey began a search for information about sexuality and, when he could find virtually none, began the research which made his name a household word throughout the United States and the world. His first book, *Sexual Behavior in the Human Male*, published in 1948, was the true beginning of the movement for sexual freedom, sometimes known as the sexual revolution, which is still going on today. Although it created a great deal of controversy, it showed people that their sexual actions were not unique, that what they did sexually was also being done by others.

In 1953 Kinsey published *Sexual Behavior in the Human Female*, a book which today ranks at the top of the list of "must" reading for those seriously interested in the field of human sexuality. Unfortunately our culture was not ready to concede that women were sexual in 1953 (it is just beginning to understand that now). A storm of protest arose over the concept that women were indeed orgasm-seeking creatures just as were men. Although Kinsey died in 1956, disillusioned about public response to his work, the institute he founded at Indiana University continues his work. The Institute for Sex Research, under the direction of Dr. Paul Gebhard, is still one of the foremost organizations in the field of sex research.

One of the important movements to influence the sex field was the humanistic psychological movement which suggested that people have as much right to feel as they do to think. Another movement which began bringing the word sex to public attention was the homosexual movement which began in California in the early 1950s and sprang to nationwide attention as the Gay Liberation movement in the mid-60s. Also in the mid-60s came the second wave of the feminist movement which has had a profound effect on relationships between people. All of these movements have one thing in common—a strong desire to see all persons treated as equals with the right to feel good about themselves and to live the lifestyle which best suits them without societal interference.

Another push to the sex field came with the publication of *Human Sexual Response* by Dr. William Masters and Virginia Johnson in 1966. This historic book, based on laboratory research on the physiology of sexual

response, did much to validate the earlier Kinsey studies and to bring sex to the attention of the medical community. In 1970 Masters and Johnson published *Human Sexual Inadequacy* which also added to our store of knowledge about human sexuality.

The search for knowledge about human beings and their sexuality continues. It sometimes seems that the more we find out the more there is to find out. As the scholars and researchers seek more information, the National Sex Forum seeks to bring that information to the people as it becomes available. We believe that it is time to say "yes" to sex.

Sex plays a very important role in every person's life. Sexual fantasies, desires, and dreams should be recognized as valuable and integral parts of each person's sexuality.

Sex can and should be discussed casually and non-judgmentally. Individuals can enrich their own sex lives by learning about the full range of sexual behavior. Individuals have a right to know all the facts.

Everyone has a right to a good sex life, including persons who have physical disabilities (paraplegics, diabetics, amputees, heart patients) or mental and emotional problems.

Sexuality is the most individualistic part of a person's life. It is up to each individual to determine and then to assume responsibility for her or his own sexuality. All of the varying modes of expression are available to everyone. As long as people know what they are doing, feel good about it, and don't harm others, anything goes.

To experience a healthy and fulfilling sex life, we need to learn about and appreciate our own bodies, know our feelings and our own sexual responses, become sensitive to the physical and emotional needs of others, and develop meaningful intimate loving contact in our sexual relationships.

The Technique Involves:

A Step by Step Training Process
A System and a Plan
Graduated Training
Mutual Working Together
Pleasuring and Being Pleasured
Success
At Home Exercises
A Journal

We feel that everyone's sexuality is unique and that it is a potentially positive, joyous, and enriching experience. We feel that each individual and couple needs to find the unique pattern that works for them. We would like you to have as full and as good a sexual life as possible.

WHAT IT TAKES TO MAKE IT WORK

You have to:

    Want to take the time to work
    Put off immediate gratification in order to have long range gratification
    Stick to it and do it

If partnered:

    Be willing to bare yourselves to each other (pun intended)

During the classes and at home, you will be:

    Talking
    Listening
    Seeing
    Sharing
    Touching
    Practicing
    Reading
    Doing at home exercises
    Planning for the future
    Learning to explore your feelings in the here and now

To get the full benefit from this program we expect you to:

    Be here now
    Take the time to do the exercises
    Do it for yourself
    Make an effort
    Be willing to substitute a program for a problem
    Be honest with yourself

SITUATIONAL ASSESSMENT

The first step in this process is for you to get a sense of where you have been. So—take your own sex history. If a question doesn't seem to apply to you skip it—or write in a word that does apply to your history.

A

PSE/E SEXUAL EXPERIENCE SURVEY, PART I

Sex _____ Age _____

Circle One or Fill in the Blanks

1. Current living status:

    Single   Married   Divorced
    Separated   Widowed   Engaged
    Living with sexual partner—not married
    Living with roommate(s)   Living alone
    Living with parents
    Other_____

2. Your living arrangements have been like this for:

    _____ months   _____ years

3. Your living arrangement is:

    Very happy   Happy   Satisfactory
    Unsatisfactory   Very unsatisfactory

4. Your occupation(s):

    _____
    _____

5. How would you rate your commitment to religious doctrines?

    None   Slight   Moderate   Strong

6. How important are religious doctrines to you?

    Not important   Good as guidelines
    Constant and unchanging
    Sacred and unchangeable

7. Your parents are:

    Living together   Widowed   Divorced
    Separated   Dead

8. Your parent's marriage is (was) successful:

    Yes   Somewhat   No

9. The sources of sex education most important to you were: (rank 1, 2, 3, etc.)

Father ____   Friends (samesex) ____
Mother ____   Friends (opsex) ____
Brother(s) ____   Youth groups ____
Sister(s) ____   Movies ____
Relatives ____   High school ____
School before high school ____
School after high school ____
Magazines and books ____

10. Do (did) your parents influence your decision-making regarding your sexual behavior?

Never   Seldom   Sometimes   Usually   Always

11. How old were you when you had your first actual date with a member of either sex?

_____ years old.   Which sex?

12. Do your friends of either or both sexes influence your decision-making regarding sexual behavior?

Never   Seldom   Sometimes   Usually   Always

13. How important would you say sexual pleasure is to you?

Very   Somewhat   Slightly   Not at all

14. In general, describe the degree to which your sexual needs are satisfied:

Much above average   Above average
About average   Below average
Much below average

15. In general, describe the degree to which you are able to express your sexual desires and concerns comfortably to others:

Much above average   Above average
About average   Below average
Much below average

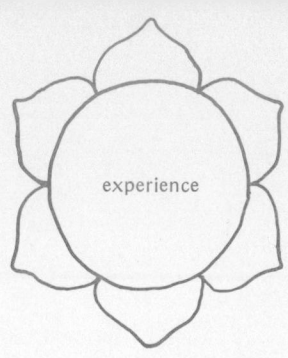

experience

16. To what extent are your associates, friends, sexual partner(s) comfortable in discussing their personal sex behavior and attitudes: Much   Somewhat   Average   Little   None   A

17. How old were you when you first fantasized about sex? _____ years old

18. How old were you when you first experienced orgasm (if ever)? _____ years old

19. How old were you when you first experienced a wet dream (if ever)? _____ years old

20. When was the last time you had a wet dream? _____ ago

21. On the average, how often do you date, or get together on a private basis with someone now?

Times per week _____   Times per month _____

Times per year _____

Number of women _____

Number of men _____

22. On the average, how many different people do you presently date or get together with on a private basis? (regardless of sexual activity)   Women _____   Men _____

23. What is your present dating status?   None   Randomly   Steady   Engaged
Other _____

24. Did you ever have a course in school which dealt with human sexual behavior?   Yes   No   When _____

19

25. The environment and circumstances of your first sexual experience can be best described as:

My parents' home with privacy
My parents' home with fear of being found out
My partner's home with privacy
My partner's home with fear of being found out
In a parked car with privacy
In a parked car with fear of being found out
Outdoors with privacy
Outdoors with fear of being found out
Other_____

26. Which statement most accurately describes your first sexual experience with a partner of either sex? Which sex _____

Looking at each other's genitals
Looking and fondling each other's genitals
Petting short of orgasm
Petting to orgasm
Rubbing own genitals against partner's genitals
Intercourse (genital-genital)
Oral-genital sexual contact
Deep kissing (making out)
Mutual masturbation
Anal intercourse
Interfemoral—penis between partner's legs
Other_____

27. How old were you at the time of your first partner-sexual experience? _____ years old

28. How old was your partner? _____ years old

29. Was this your partner's first such experience? Yes   No

30. How old were you when you first had intercourse? _____ years old

31. Was this your partner's first intercourse experience? Yes   No

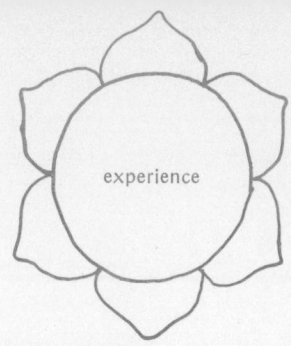

experience

32. During your first partner-sexual experience, were you: Active   Passive   As active as partner

33. The partner in your first sexual experience was:

A friend(s)   Sibling(s)   Father
Mother   Uncle   Aunt
Stranger   Cousin   Neighbor
Casual acquaintance   Prostitute
A love relationship
Surrogate   Other _____

34. What is the greatest number of times you have experienced orgasm during any one 24-hour period?

_____

35. During your most active 24 hours, rank (1, 2, 3, etc.) the most important actions utilized to achieve orgasm:

Intercourse ____   Oral-genital ____
Petting ____   Masturbated myself ____
Fantasy ____   Mutual masturbation ____
Dreaming ____   Anal intercourse ____
Interfemoral sex (under or between legs) ____
Other _____

36. During your most active 24 hours, how many different partners did you have?

____ Women   ____ Men

37. How old were you the first time you masturbated (to orgasm)?

____ years old

38. During the last year, how often have you masturbated (to orgasm)?

_____/week   _____/month   _____/year

39. When you masturbated this year, did you enjoy it?

Always   Mostly   Sometimes   Rarely   Never

21

40. Have you masturbated with a vibrator, dildo, or other device?　　　Frequently　　Sometimes　　Rarely　　Never

41. Do you fantasize when you masturbate?　　　Frequently　　Sometimes　　Rarely　　Never

42. Do you fantasize while having sexual relations with your partner?　　　Frequently　　Sometimes　　Rarely　　Never

43. During the last year, how many different people have you had sexual experiences with?　　　_____

44. During the past year, how many different people have you had intercourse with?　　　_____

45. During the past year, how often, on the average, have you had sexual intercourse?　　　____times a week　　____times a month

46. This frequency was _____ than you would prefer.　　　More often　　Satisfactory　　Less often

47. When you had sexual intercourse during the past year, was it something that you enjoyed?　　　Always　　Mostly　　Sometimes　　Rarely　　Never

48. Do you enjoy sexual intercourse more or less than you used to?　　　More　　Less

49. How many different sex partners have you had during your life up until now?　　　_____ (rough estimate okay)

50. How many different sex partners did you have before you were first married (if ever)?　　　_____ (rough estimate okay)

51. How many different sex partners have you had since living with your partner?　　　_____ (rough estimate okay)

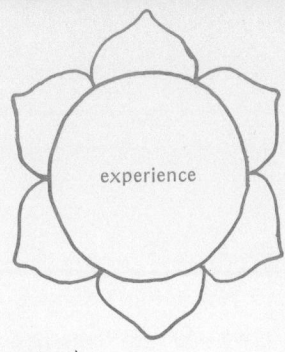

experience

52. How many times, if ever, have you had sexual interaction with a prostitute?   _____ (rough estimate okay)

A

53. What age persons do you have as sexual partners?

In order of frequency (1, 2, 3, etc.)

0-12 ____   26-35 ____
13-17 ____   36-45 ____
18-25 ____   46-60 ____
              over 60 ____

54. Have you ever seen or read anything specifically about human sexual behavior, such as books, journals, pornography, erotic literature, photographs, pictures, films, etc?   Yes   No

55. If yes, indicate by circling above and listing representative titles:

_____
_____
_____
_____

56. Rank in order the most important reasons for reading/looking at the above materials:

Erotic purposes ____
Curiosity ____
Information ____
Amusement ____
Other ____

57. Have you ever been raped, forced, or coerced into sexual activity?   Yes   No

58. Have you ever raped, forced, or coerced anyone into sexual activity?   Yes   No

59. Have you ever fantasized about raping or being raped?   Yes   No

60. Have you ever let an animal give you sexual pleasure?   Yes   No

61. Have you ever masturbated an animal?   Yes   No

62. Have you ever used an animal for sexual pleasure?   Yes   No

63. Would you *now*:
    Let an animal give you pleasure?   Yes   No
    Give an animal sexual pleasure?   Yes   No
    Use an animal for sexual pleasure?   Yes   No

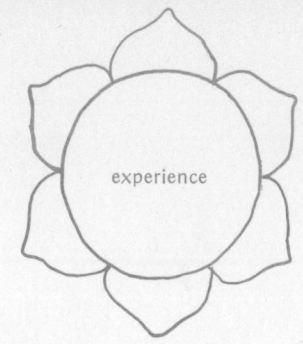

PSE/E SEXUAL EXPERIENCE SURVEY, PART II. FANTASY

People frequently think about or try to imagine different sexual activities, even if they have never experienced them. For each kind of sexual activity listed, please indicate your reaction *if* you have ever *thought of* or *considered experiencing* that activity.

ACTIVITIES	Aroused	Interested	Informed	Curious	Amused	Accepting	Uncomfortable	Shocked	Disgusted
Coitus									
Oral-genital contact									
Lesbian contact									
Male homosexual contact									
Group sex									
Sado-masochistic sex									
Sex with animals									
Anal sex									

Whether or not you have previously thought of or considered the sexual acts in the previous items, what is your reaction to fantasizing these activities now?

ACTIVITIES	Very erotic	Somewhat erotic	Neither erotic nor a turnoff	Somewhat of a turnoff	Definitely a turnoff
Coitus					
Oral-genital contact					
Lesbian contact					
Male homosexual contact					
Group sex					
Sado-masochistic sex					
Sex with animals					
Anal sex					

PSE/E SEXUAL EXPERIENCE SURVEY, PART III

Have you ever tried any one of the following activities?

ACTIVITIES	With Opposite Sex		With Same Sex	
	Yes	No	Yes	No
Oral-genital contact (active)				
Oral-genital contact (passive)				
Anal intercourse (active)				
Anal intercourse (passive)				
Group sex				
Sex with a much younger person				
Sex with a much older person				
Sadism				
Masochism				
Nude massage (active)				
Nude massage (passive)				

For those activities that you tried, check the word that describes the degree to which you enjoyed them.

ACTIVITIES WITH OPPOSITE SEX	Very much	Somewhat	Not too much	Not at all
Oral-genital contact (active)				
Oral-genital contact (passive)				
Anal intercourse (active)				
Anal intercourse (passive)				
Group sex				
Sex with a much younger person				
Sex with a much older person				
Sadism				
Masochism				
Nude massage (active)				
Nude massage (passive)				

experience

A

ACTIVITIES WITH SAME SEX	Very much	Somewhat	Not too much	Not at all
Oral-genital contact (active)				
Oral-genital contact (passive)				
Anal intercourse (active)				
Anal intercourse (passive)				
Group sex				
Sex with a much younger person				
Sex with a much older person				
Sadism				
Masochism				
Nude massage (active)				
Nude massage (passive)				

For those activities that you enjoyed, check the answers which describe the *reasons* you enjoyed them:

ACTIVITIES WITH OPPOSITE SEX	Activity was erotic	Circumstances were erotic	Partner was erotic	Regular part of lifestyle	I was just horny
Oral-genital contact (active)					
Oral-genital contact (passive)					
Anal intercourse (active)					
Anal intercourse (passive)					
Group sex					
Sex with a much younger person					
Sex with a much older person					
Sadism					
Masochism					
Nude massage (active)					
Nude massage (passive)					

ACTIVITIES WITH SAME SEX	Activity was erotic	Circumstances were erotic	Partner was erotic	Regular part of lifestyle	I was just horny
Oral-genital contact (active)					
Oral-genital contact (passive)					
Anal intercourse (active)					
Anal intercourse (passive)					
Group sex					
Sex with a much younger person					
Sex with a much older person					
Sadism					
Masochism					
Nude massage (active)					
Nude massage (passive)					

Check the reasons for *not* enjoying the activities which you have tried but did not enjoy.

ACTIVITIES WITH OPPOSITE SEX	Activity not stimulating	Circumstances not stimulating	Partner not stimulating	Too unusual for me	Enjoyed at time, but now feel guilty	It hurt	Strong guilt feelings
Oral-genital contact (active)							
Oral-genital contact (passive)							
Anal intercourse (active)							
Anal intercourse (passive)							
Group sex							
Sex with a much younger person							
Sex with a much older person							
Sadism							
Masochism							
Nude massage (active)							
Nude massage (passive)							

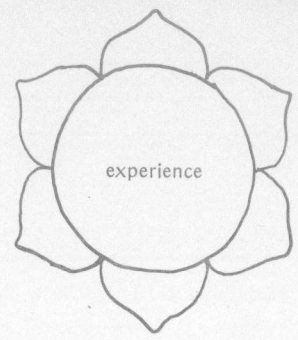

ACTIVITIES WITH SAME SEX	Activity not stimulating	Circumstances not stimulating	Partner not stimulating	Too unusual for me	Enjoyed at time, but now feel guilty	It hurt	Strong guilt feelings
Oral-genital contact (active)							
Oral-genital contact (passive)							
Anal intercourse (active)							
Anal intercourse (passive)							
Group sex							
Sex with a much younger person							
Sex with a much older person							
Sadism							
Masochism							
Nude massage (active)							
Nude massage (passive)							

Additional comments about current sexual lifestyles and/or partner relationships that were not covered in the history:

A

MY CONTRACT FOR THIS PROGRAM

Looking for change quite naturally brings some confusing and/or conflicting feelings. It takes courage and commitment to learn new things. It is very important to be willing and agreeable to do some exploring for and of yourself.

Define for yourself, in the space below, what you are committed to working on while using the SARguide. If your partner is also taking this course, what are the things that you and your partner are committed to working on together? What are some of your worries about making a commitment to this program? What will be scary about making the current situation "better"? (or different?) List three good reasons for not changing anything at all.

YOUR JOURNAL

Some pages in this book provide places for written at home exercises. It will be important to keep an additional notebook. Your own book can be the backs of old envelopes kept in a shoe box, a leather book—anything that fits your unique taste.

A

Your journal is a mirror of your own inner reflections. Writing is a way to express to yourself, and to others if you wish, your thoughts and feelings while you experience Personal Sexual Enrichment/Education (PSE/E).

Allow at least five minutes each day, preferably at the same hour, to make your journal entries. Write as much or as little as you like—whatever you feel is important—do note your reactions to the classes and visual materials, the at home exercises, and anything else you think is relevant. Tell it to yourself, how your body is feeling, how your mind is thinking.

Enter into your journal any suggestions you may have for yourself and any statements you may wish to make to others either now or at some future time.

Use pictures, phrases, feelings. Use colors, pen, pencil—whatever helps you get it out. A simple picture may describe some things better and more easily than words.

Don't let the journal slip your mind. Keep it up to date, it is an important part of this program. Later it will serve to show you the progress you have made.

Your notebook is only for you. You are not writing for a grade. Your word, phrase or picture is more important than punctuation or grammar. From time to time reread your journal. Are you being as specific and honest as you can be?

AT HOME EXERCISES

To Do Before First Group Session

	Section A Page No.
1. Taking time and space for yourself	33
2. Breathing Exercises	
a. Abdominal breathing	34
b. Synchronous breathing	35
c. Coordinated breathing	35
d. Genital focus	35
e. Complete breath	36
f. Alternate nostril breathing	36
g. Chest expansion	37
h. Pelvic breathing	38
i. Spoon breathing	39
3. Sensory Awareness	
a. "Rag Doll"	40
b. Pelvic tension breaker	40
c. Backward bend	41
d. Side bend	42
4. Kegel exercises	43
5. Body imagery—how we see ourselves	45
6. Reread "How to use the SARguide"	6

Before your first group session read through page 62 of this guide.

AT HOME EXERCISE I. TAKING TIME AND SPACE FOR YOURSELF

Find an hour that will fit comfortably into your schedule and lifestyle and claim it for yourself. These suggestions may help:

A

1. Have a frank discussion with your partner, yourself, or your housemates about respecting the hour you take for yourself.
2. Discuss the need for privacy with your children. ("Don't bother me unless it is a real emergency.")
3. Put a lock or slide-bolt on the bedroom door.
4. Put a sign on the bedroom door that says "Do Not Disturb."
5. Take a realistic look at your daily activities so you can evaluate priorities in taking time for yourself.
6. Reschedule your household duties or get another household member to share them with you.
7. Make a place in your home (or wherever you spend the most time) that is sexy, sensual, soft, and quiet.
8. Do the at home exercises each day at a regular hour (take no more than one hour).
9. Practice the sensory awareness and breathing exercises at a regular time each day, not more than ten minutes.

Only you can make it happen the way you want it to happen.

MY HOUR EACH DAY IS GOING TO BE _____.

AT HOME EXERCISE 2 — LEARNING TO BREATHE

Breathing, like sexual response, is a naturally occurring event in the body. We are often unaware of the rate and rhythm of our breathing, but some awareness of our breathing is important to sexual functioning (both general and specific). The following exercises will help you to purify, relax, and harmonize your body.

Do the exercises in the small, quiet, private space you have set aside for yourself. Your space should contain a seat in which you can sit comfortably with your spine straight, at whatever height is most comfortable. The space should be as mentally and physically comfortable as you can make it.

Abdominal Breathing — 2a

The purpose of this exercise is to develop comfortable and relaxed breathing into the pelvic region. (This is called abdominal or diaphragm breathing.)

Begin by lying on the floor or a bed with arms at your side and legs uncrossed. A small pillow under the head or neck might help make you more comfortable. Close your eyes and begin breathing slowly, inhaling through the nose and exhaling through the mouth.

Now place one hand lightly on your lower abdomen. Concentrate on the movement of your abdomen as you breathe. Push your hand upwards with your abdomen as you inhale, letting the abdomen fall as you exhale. Now, breathe in slowly, and as you exhale, use your hand to push your breath out further than you normally do. Imagine the air slowly filling your abdomen and emptying with a whoosh or sigh. Exhale at the same rate as you inhale.

Make sure your exhale more fully than you normally do. Pause after each exhalation and don't rush. Do this ten times. How often do you allow your belly to stick out!!

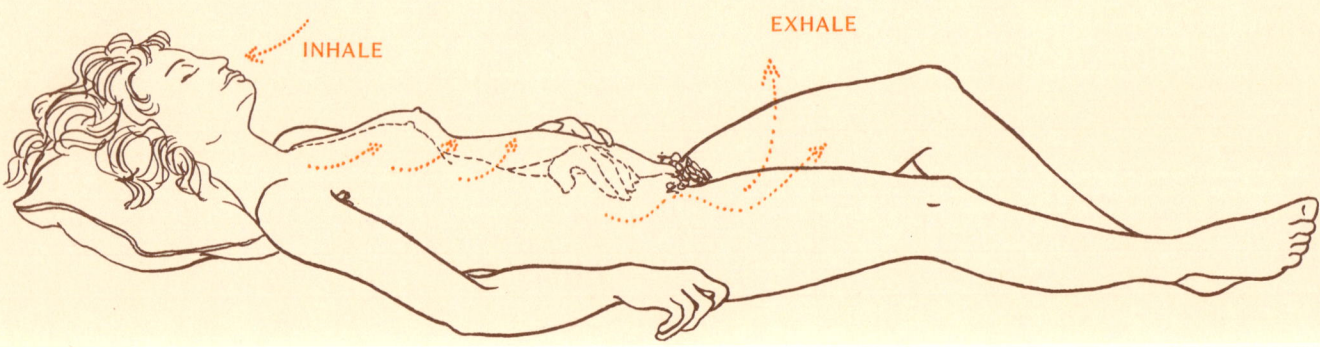

Synchronous Breathing — 2b

This exercise is designed to harmonize your breathing and heart rate. Many people find that coordinating these two important rhythms brings an increased sense of well being.

As you inhale, count the beats of your pulse; this is your breathing number. Write it down here: _____ . The number may change. Use this one for the exercises in breathing.

> Inhale to your number.
> Hold for one-half of your number.
> Exhale to your number.
> Hold for one-half your number.

As you develop a feeling for this synchronous breathing technique, your body sensations and your breathing rate will begin to change and harmonize with your pulse rate. Continue breathing in this way for three minutes each time or until you feel your heart pulse and breathing have stabilized and synchronized. Do not work for more than 10 minutes total to start with.

Coordinated Breathing — 2c

The purpose of this exercise is to develop awareness of your body while practicing relaxed breathing. By experiencing specific body movements coordinated with deep breathing you will learn how to continue deep breathing while engaged in sexual activity. Continue deep abdominal breathing, and as you inhale, turn your right foot out to the side. As you exhale, turn your right foot back up so the toes point to the ceiling. Do this six times and then switch to the left foot. Turn the left foot out to the side as you inhale, then return to start as you exhale. Do this six times.

Repeat the exercise sequence again, first with the right hand, then with the left. Raise the hand slightly and inhale, lowering it as you exhale. Repeat six times.

Genital Focus Breathing — 2d

Breathe in through your nose and then imagine that you are breathing out through a four inch diameter pipe in your genitals! "Exhale through your crotch." Repeat this six times, eyes closed.

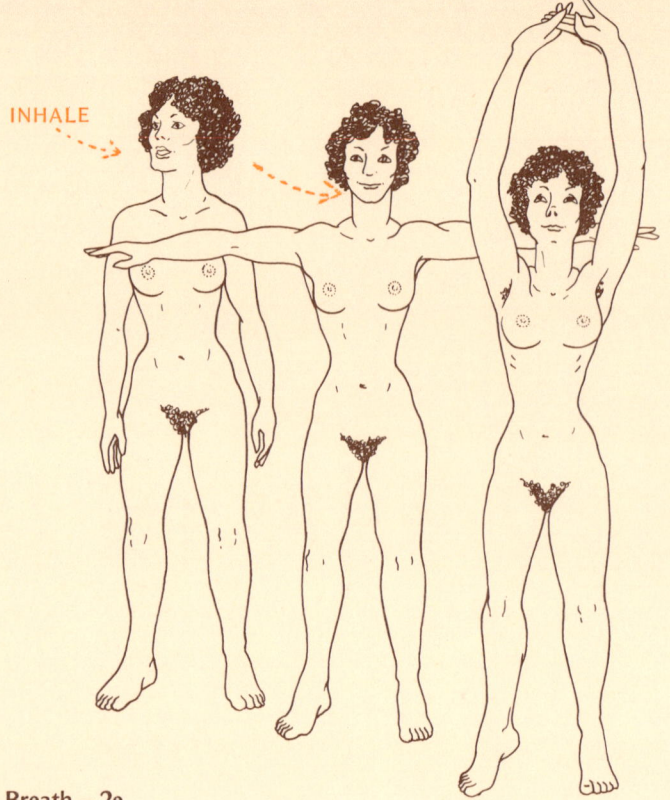

Complete Breath — 2e

1. Stand easily and erectly with arms at sides. Exhale through your nose; empty the lungs completely.
2. Slowly inhale through the nose to a count of nine. As you inhale first push out your abdomen and then your entire chest.
3. While inhaling slowly bring your arms overhead and simultaneously rise on toes. Count nine to complete movements 2 and 3. Touch palms overhead at count of nine. Hold for a moment.
4. Slowly exhale through your nose to a count of nine; as you exhale, lower your arms slowly and return heels to floor.
5. Repeat without pause, 4 to 10 times.

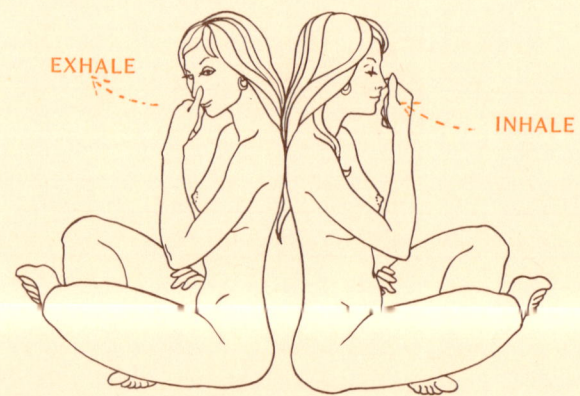

Alternate Nostril Breathing — 2f

1. Stand easily and erectly, feet apart or sit in a comfortable position with back straight.
2. Place the thumb and first finger of your left hand on the side of each nostril. Exhale.
3. Close left nostril with thumb; inhale through right nostril to a count of nine, first pushing out abdomen and then entire chest.
4. Close right nostril with forefinger; exhale through left nostril to count of nine. Do each side 3 to 10 times.
5. Repeat; inhaling through left nostril and exhaling through right nostril.
6. Repeat, always inhaling and exhaling through alternate nostrils.

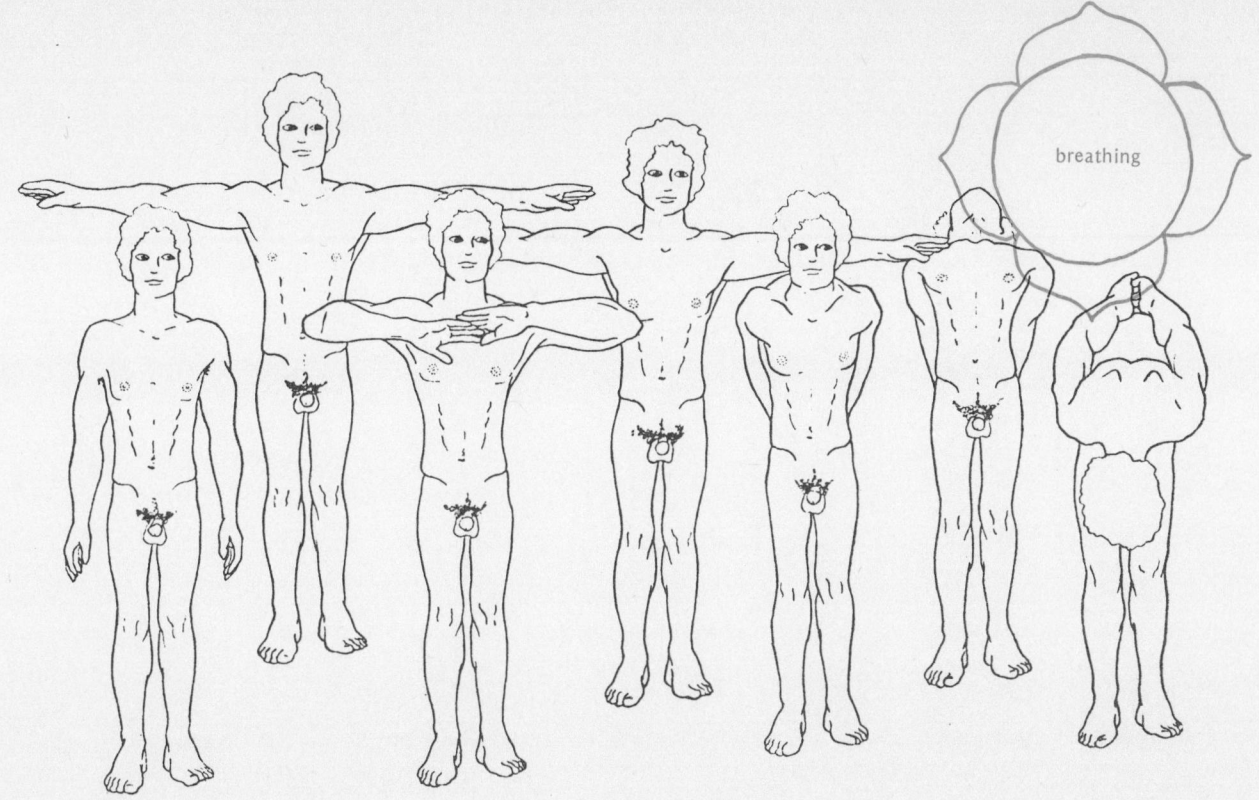

Chest Expansion—2g

1. Stand easily and erectly; slowly raise arms to shoulder level. Bend elbows, bringing hands in to touch chest, palms outward.
2. Move arms out and straighten back as far as possible without strain. Clasp hands and straighten arms. Count five for each of these movements.
3. Gently bend backward from waist as far as possible without strain. Hold.
4. Bring clasped hands, arms straight, up over back and bend forward as far as possible. Relax neck and hold.
5. Slowly straighten up. Unclasp hands. Relax.

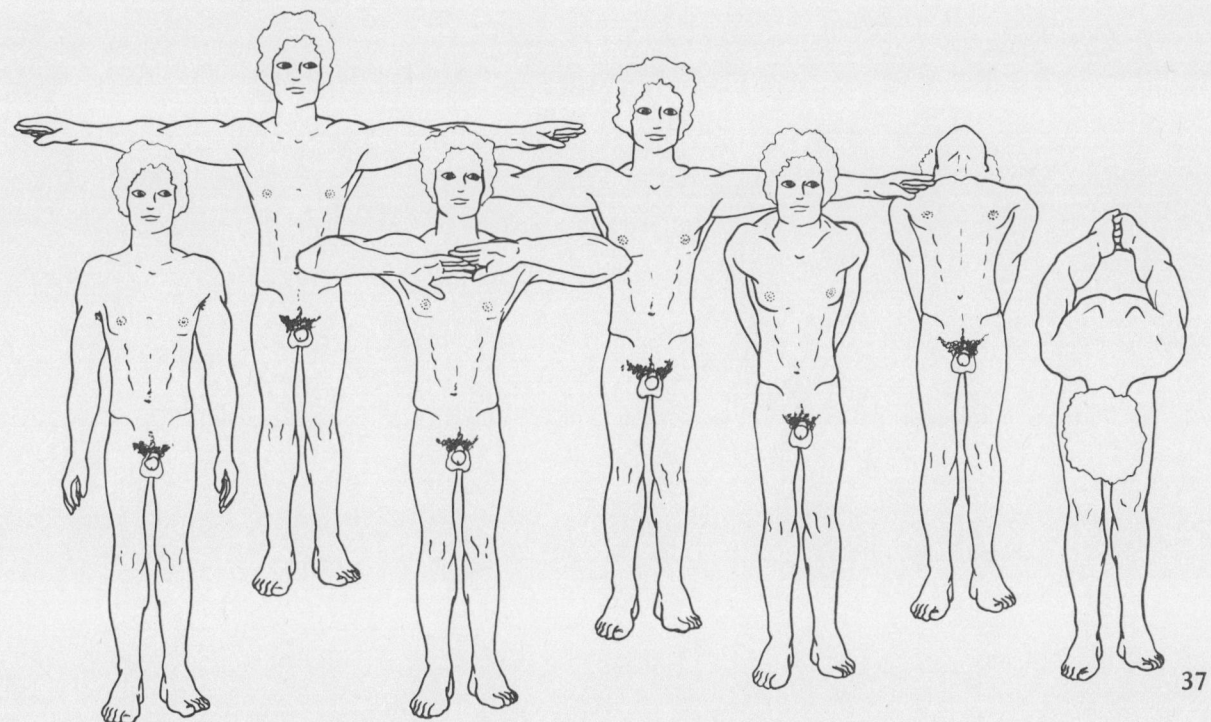

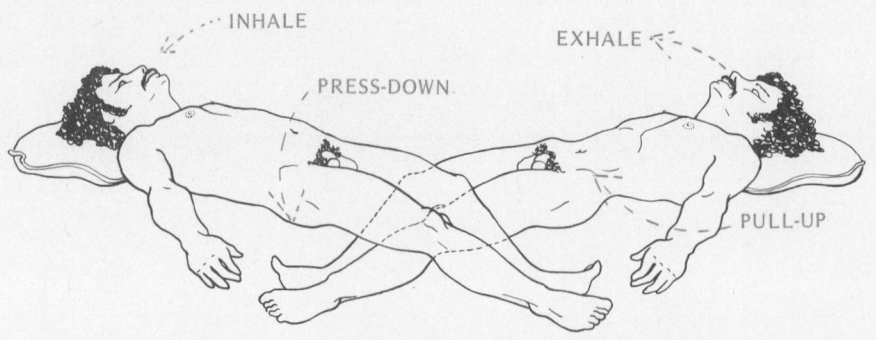

Pelvic Breathing — 2h

The purpose of this breathing exercise is to begin to coordinate pelvic movement with breathing.

Lay down on your back on the floor or bed with arms at your sides and legs uncrossed. Breathe slowly, using abdominal breathing for a few minutes to establish your rhythm. Close your eyes. As you inhale, press your bottom towards the floor and let the air fill your abdomen. As you exhale, imagine that your pubic bone is being magnetically drawn towards the ceiling. The magnet is attached right to the clitoris or penis. Your pelvis will slowly tilt up as you exhale. Repeat this at least ten times. It is important to have the pelvis tilt backwards on the inhalation and tilt forward on the exhalation. The abdomen continues to fill out as you push your bottom down towards the floor.

Do the same exercise while kneeling with your hands flat on the floor in front of you. As you inhale, push your bottom towards the ceiling and let your belly hang down low at the same time. Arms are still. As you exhale, push your pelvic bone towards the floor, forward. Repeat this six times.

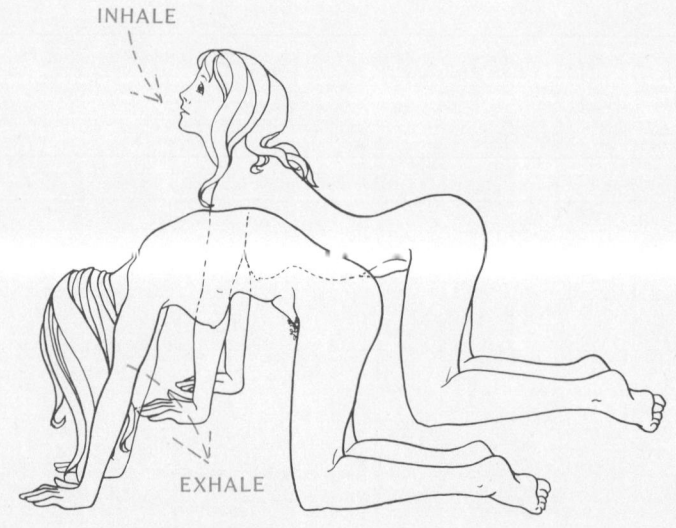

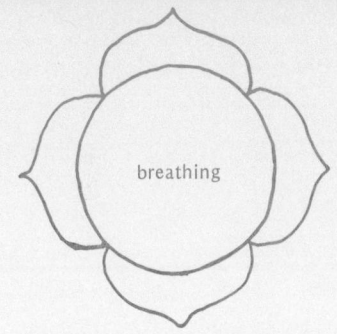

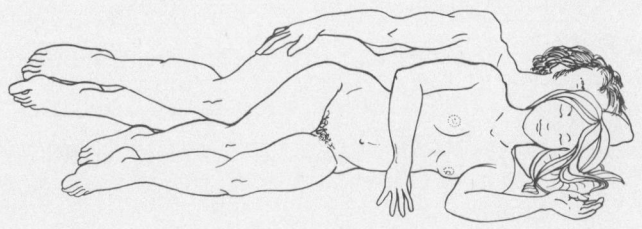

"Spoon" Breathing — 2i

People in relationships of any sort often move and act at different paces and in different rhythms. How often do you feel in harmony with your partner? Doing a breathing exercise with your partner can increase your awareness of your own and his/her body rhythm.

1. Lie on your sides very close together and facing the same direction. Your bodies ought to look like spoons lying together in a drawer.
2. Breathe at your own pace for a few moments and feel yourselves begin to relax.
3. When you feel relaxed, the person in the *back* position starts to follow the breathing rhythm of the person in the *front*. Try to breathe at the same pace as your partner for ten minutes.
4. Switch places or turn in the other direction and the new person in back follow the breathing of the person in front.

Don't talk during the entire twenty minutes. It's best to do this exercise when you are *not* about ready to go to sleep.

After you have both had a turn at leading and following, discuss the experience. Did you feel closer or more distant? Were you more comfortable leading or following? Are you aware of other ways you lead and follow each other?

AT HOME EXERCISE 3 — SENSORY AWARENESS

The following are helpful for developing the ability to relax and for increasing body awareness. They are simple and take little time. While doing the exercises, concentrate on the changes taking place in your body. If you should find extraneous thoughts entering your mind (work, the world, etc.) merely let them pass through and return to focusing on the body.

"Rag Doll" — 3a

1. Stand with feet apart. The distance of one foot from the other should approximate the distance from shoulder to shoulder.
2. Lean forward from the waist, allowing your arms, neck, and head to dangle from your trunk. Don't force your fingertips closer to the floor. Allow the upper portion of your body to go limp. Repeat three to five times.

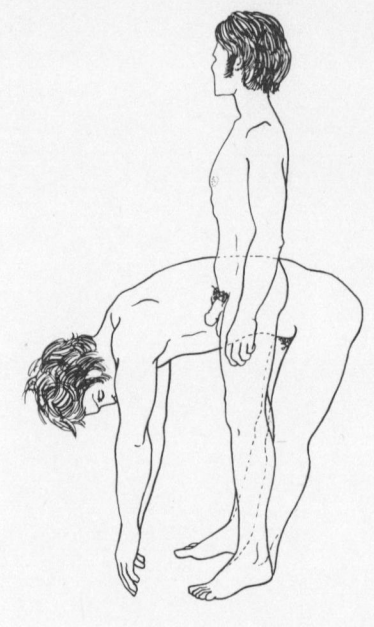

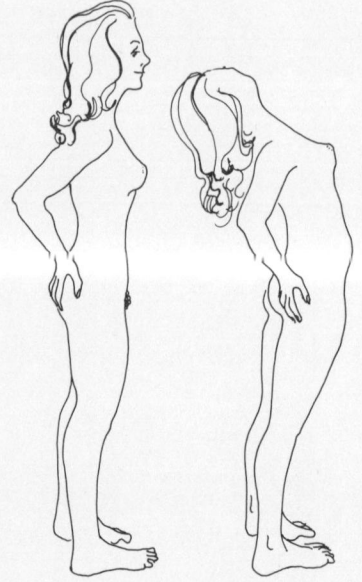

Pelvic Tension Breaker — 3b

1. Stand easily and erectly; place your fists just below your waist in back; place feet apart at shoulder distance from each other with toes pointing inward.
2. Slowly arch your back; press fists into pelvis using as much pressure as possible; allow head and neck to fall backward.
3. Rock back and forth between heels and toes, increasing pressure of fists with each movement until maximum amount of pressure is being exerted on your pelvis.
4. Return feet to position flat on floor. Hold to count of five.
5. Slowly return to standing. Relax. Repeat three to five times.

exercises

Backward Bend — 3c

(Count "5" for all movements. Perform three times.)
1. Sit on heels. Keep knees on the floor and touch finger tips to the floor just to the side of and slightly behind each foot.
2. *Slowly* move hands or fingertips back to a comfortable distance behind you.
3. *Slowly* raise trunk to form an arch, staying seated on heels. Drop head back. Hold this position.
4. *Slowly* relax trunk. Rest in position two.

Side Bend — 3d

(Count five for all movements. Perform three to five times each side.)
1. Stand erect, feet apart. Raise arms at sides to shoulder level, palms facing downward.
2. Slowly bend to left side from waist; keep knees straight. Bring right arm overhead; slide left hand down the side of left leg as far as is comfortable. Allow neck to go limp.
3. Slowly straighten up.
4. Repeat to the right.

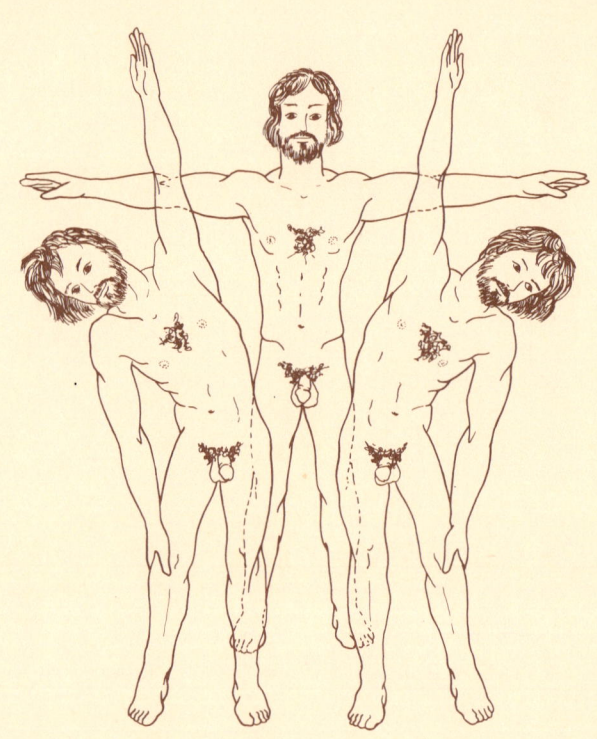

AT HOME EXERCISE 4 — KEGEL EXERCISES

These exercises are designed to strengthen and give you voluntary control over a muscle called the Pubococcygeus muscle—(pew-bo-kak-se-gee-us), or P.C. for short. This muscle is the support muscle for the genitals in both men and women. There is a definite correlation between good tone in the P.C. muscle and orgasmic intensity.

A

These exercises can help you to:

1. Increase your awareness of feelings in your genital area.
2. Increase blood circulation in the genital area.
3. Add to your sexual responsiveness.
4. Aid in restoring vaginal muscle tone following childbirth.
5. Increase your control over your orgasm.

To find your P.C. muscle, when you need to urinate, see if you can start and stop the flow of urine with your legs apart (without moving your legs together). The P.C. muscle is the one that stops the flow.

If you don't find it the first time, don't give up; try again the next time you need to urinate. Men can stand.

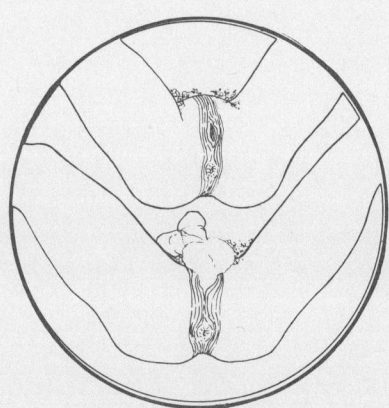

43

Slow Kegels — 4a

Tighten the P.C. muscle and hold it as you did when you stopped the flow of urine for a slow count of 3. Then relax the muscle.

Quick Kegels — 4b

Tighten and relax the P.C. muscle as rapidly as you can. At first it will feel like a flutter. You will gradually gain more control.

Pull In / Push Out — 4c

Pull up the entire pelvic area as though trying to suck up water into the genitals. Then push out or bear down as if trying to push the imaginary water out. (This exercise will use a number of "stomach" or "abdominal" muscles as well as the P.C. muscle.)

Repetitions

At first do *ten* of these exercises (one set), 3 times a day (3 exercises x 10 times x 3 times a day = 90 total exercises to start).

Each week add *5 more times* to each exercise. Example: Week 2 — 3 sets x *15 times* x 3 times a day; Week 3 — 3 sets x *20 times* x 3 times a day; Week 4 — 3 sets x *25 times* x 3 times a day. Keep doing 3 sets a day.

You can help yourself remember to do the exercises by associating them with some activity you do every day: talking on the phone, watching television, waiting in line, or lying in bed. Think of activities which don't require much moving around.

Don't worry if your muscles seem to get tired easily at first; that's normal for exercising any new muscle group. Rest between sets for a few seconds and start again. Remember to keep breathing naturally.

Women can place one or two fingers into the vagina and men one finger on each side of the base of the penis in order to feel the movement and strength of the muscle. You may also watch the movement by looking at your genitals in a hand mirror. Doing these things with your Kegels will help you learn them more rapidly.

AT HOME EXERCISE 5 — BODY IMAGERY

Begin your hour with a shower or bath—not just to get clean, but to experience rubbing soap and your hands all over your body (no wash cloth, please). This is a time to relax and begin to focus on your body.

Look at your body closely in a full-length mirror. Experience seeing your whole body, front and back. Look with your eyes and with your hands. Look at your body from different positions: sitting, kneeling, squatting, standing, bending. You can move around and play, too.

Apply a lotion or oil all over your body. Feel the different textures, muscles and bones. Discover which parts you like to look at and touch and which parts you don't like. Discover which parts you like to stroke and which you don't.

How does your attitude toward your body influence your behavior? What about the part of your body you are hiding? How do you hide it? What about the part of your body you are proud of? How do you stress that part of your body?

Where do your models for physical attractiveness come from? Your mother? Men? A man? Your own feelings? *Vogue* Magazine?

What parts of your body do you associate with pleasure?
How do you stimulate them?
What parts do you associate with pain?
How do you deal with those parts?
What parts don't you like and why not?
How much do you feel that people only like or dislike you for your body?
Can you allow yourself to look lousy sometimes and feel people will like you anyhow?
Do you feel that your appearance really expresses who you are?
What qualities would you like your body to communicate?
Do you allow yourself or your partner to touch the parts you don't like:
How do you feel when these parts are stroked or looked at?

AT HOME EXERCISE 6 — READING AHEAD FOR NEXT SESSION

Reread "How to Use this SARguide", p. 6

Anatomy and Physiology of the Sexual Response Cycle, p. 49

Fantasy. p. 56

Masturbation, p. 59

Sensate Focus, p. 62

Journal Reminder
How did you feel about the: sex history? at home exercises?

IMPRESSIONS

MANTRA

May the warm sun shine all around you
All love surround you
And the pure light within you
Guide your way home

I have two friends: my Cunt, my Death,
   Winged, Hooded, always with me
      —CS

NAVAHO PRAYER

Peaceful   Before me peaceful
              Behind me peaceful
              Over me peaceful
              Under me peaceful
              All around me
                            peaceful

Biting is described by Van de Velde as, often, "a wish to give a kiss more intense than is humanly possible; to make a permanent impression." Our oral sex drives are very closely associated with the rewarding experience of early childhood: sucking at the breast or bottle; seeing, touching, and finally placing an object in the mouth.

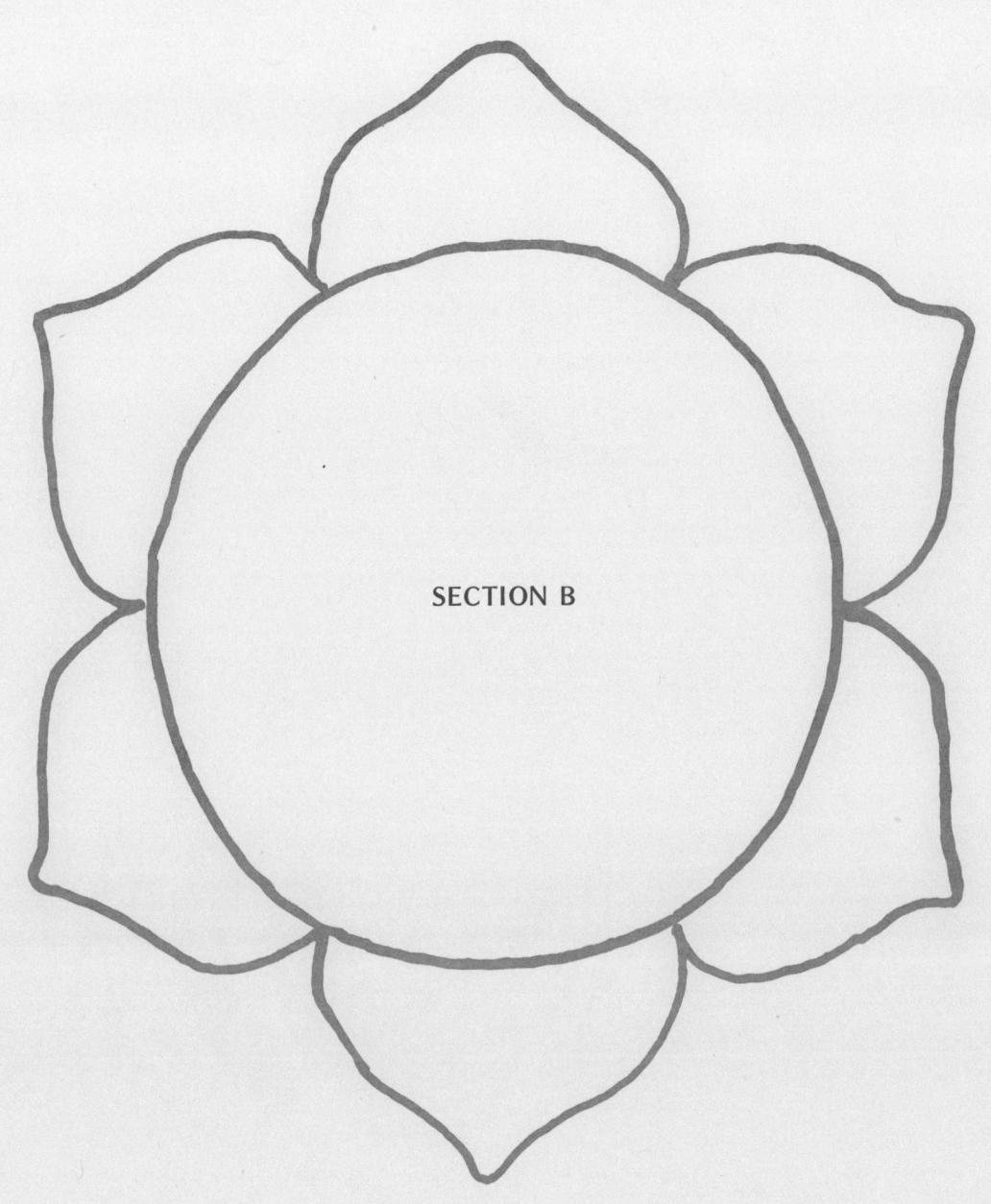
SECTION B

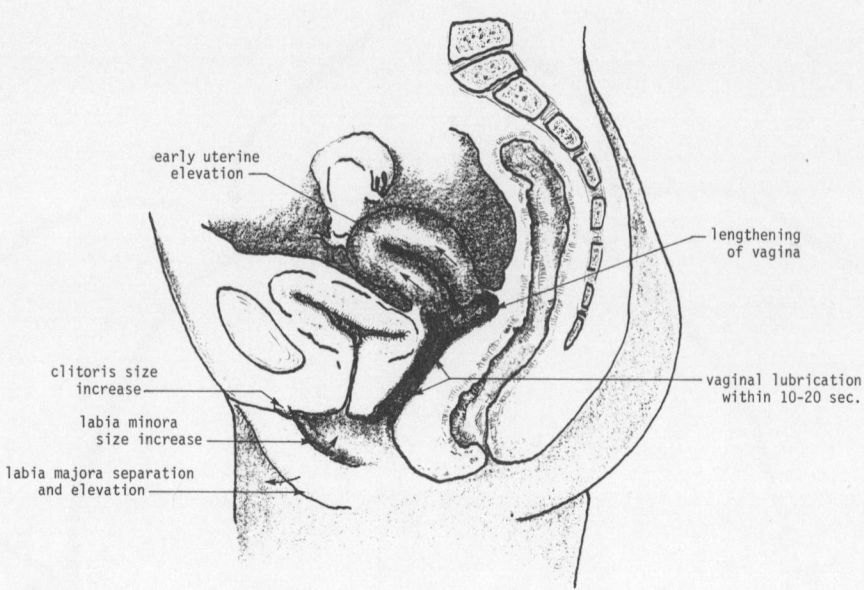

Female pelvis: excitement phase

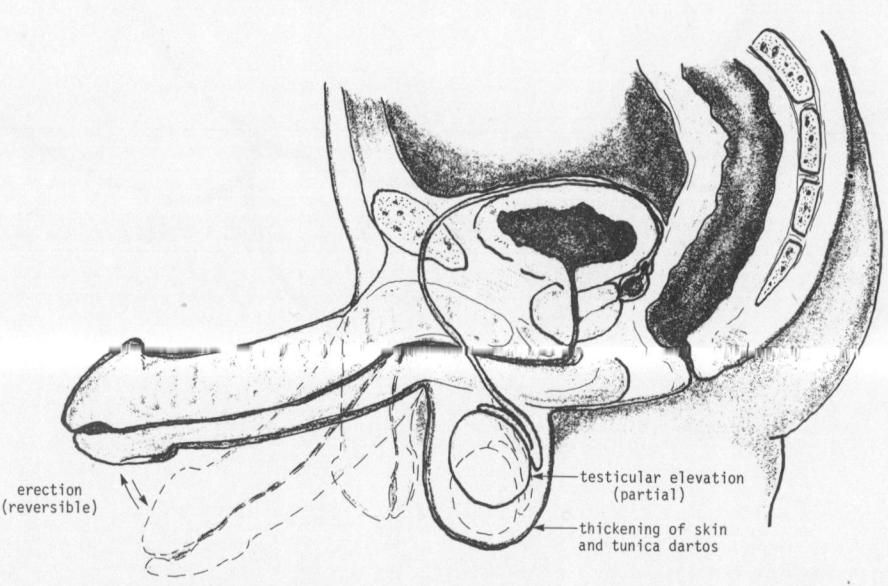

Male pelvis: excitement phase

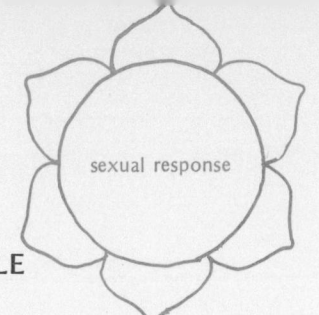

ANATOMY AND PHYSIOLOGY OF THE SEXUAL RESPONSE CYCLE

The Sexual Response Cycle is a model used to illustrate physical changes the body goes through in responding to sexual stimuli. The cycle is a continuum, and can be seen as a series of stages. Our bodies go through the response cycle in the same way regardless of the type of activity engaged in (oral, manual, coital, etc.). We may go through all or part of the cycle.

The cycle, first described in modern times by Wilhelm Reich, is generally acknowledged to consist of four general phases, occurring along an unspecified timeline. Reich described these phases as mechanical tension, bioelectric charge, bioelectric discharge, and mechanical relaxation.

More recently, Johnson and Masters re-labeled these phases: excitement, plateau, orgasm, resolution. In addition, they introduced the concept of a refractory period, the fifth phase of the sexual response cycle.

PHASE I. EXCITEMENT/MECHANICAL TENSION

We get turned on through our senses—seeing, feeling, touching, smelling, tasting, hearing—and through thought or fantasy. An impulse is generated within the body in response to something happening outside or in the mind. The body wants to act in some manner to express this impulse.

The physiological manifestations at Phase I of the sexual response cycle are: changes in blood pressure, pulse, and respiration rate; and vasocongestion or engorgement with blood; muscle tension. Sexual arousal is first noticeable as the blood supply to the abdomen and pelvic areas increases.

Female

In the woman, sexual arousal is usually manifested by vaginal lubrication, blood engorgement, and sweating of the vaginal walls. The clitoris (made up of a glans and shaft similar to the penis) swells. The shaft of the clitoris extends about an inch under the skin and is generally not seen. The glans of the clitoris is packed with sensitive nerve endings, and is covered with a retractable hood. The hood is attached to the inner lips surrounding the vagina. In sexual arousal, swelling of the glans and an increase in the diameter of the shaft of the clitoris occurs, and some swelling of the inner lips takes place. This swelling makes the vaginal barrel somewhat longer. Excitement continues. The walls of the vaginal barrel begin to balloon out and back.

Male

In the man an erection usually occurs. The penis fills with blood. The penis enlarges and stands at an angle to the body. The tip, or glans, becomes extremely sensitive and red. The scrotum and testicles pull up towards the body.

Other changes may occur in either sex: nipple erection, sex flush on the abdomen and spreading upwards, increase in pulse (or heart) rate, increased breathing rate, rise in blood pressure. Muscles continue to build up tension.

Psychologically, at this point a decision is made for or against engaging in some sexual action. The considerations are usually "Shall I be alone, with someone," "wait till I marry," etc. The decision to engage in some sexual action, either alone or with someone else, is made consciously. (Where this conscious consensuality is not present and some sexual action is engaged in, some coercion or violation of the other has occurred.)

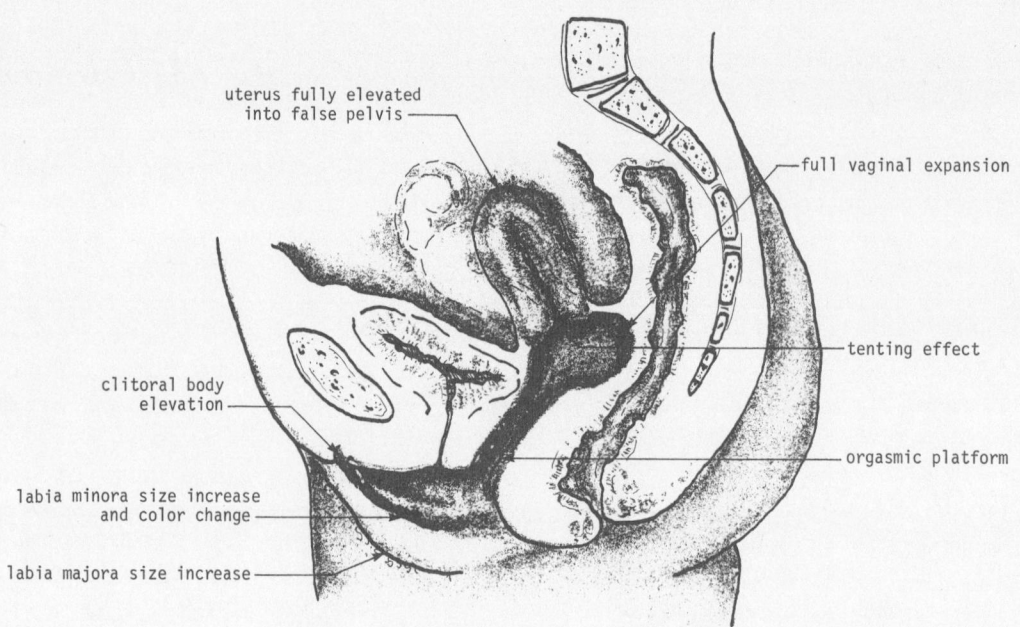

Female pelvis: plateau phase

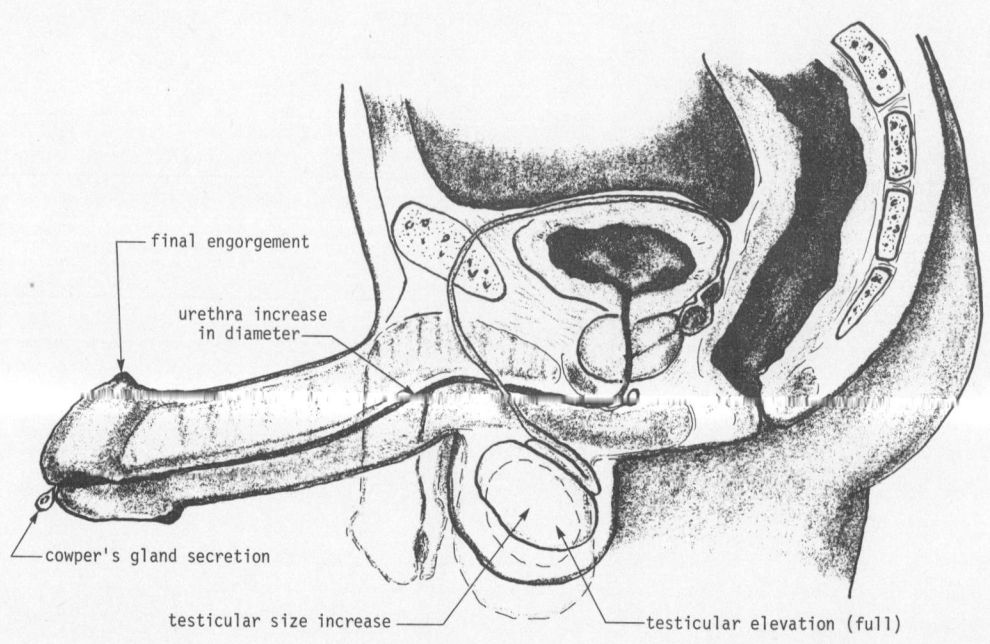

Male pelvis: plateau phase

PHASE II. PLATEAU/BIOELECTRIC CHARGE

We do something sexual. We begin active sexual movements and feel the flow of pleasurable feelings centering in the genitals and abdomen. The entire body is gradually flooded with warmth, generally increasing in intensity and reaching toward a peak.

In both sexes, heart rate, breathing rate and flushing (if it occurs) continue to increase. The tension in the musculature increases (in involuntary as well as voluntary muscles).

Female

During this phase in women, formation of the "orgasmic platform" in the outer third of the vagina occurs. Contraction of the vaginal muscles can grip the penis or a finger quite firmly. The outer lips swell even more at this stage, while the inner lips become even more deeply colored (red). The clitoris usually elevates or retracts and its shaft shortens so that the clitoris may be hard to find. The uterus is pulled upward into the abdomen (a few inches) enlarging still further the total vaginal barrel.

Male

The penis reaches fullest erection and enlargement of the coronal ridge occurs. The testicles have increased in size by about 50 percent and are pulled up tightly by further shortening of the (internal) spermatic cords. Full elevation of the testicles is a sign that the man has reached "the point of no return" where ejaculation is imminent. A few drops of clear liquid may appear at the opening of the penis; this is a secretion from Cowper's gland. This pre-ejaculate may contain some live sperm although the main function of the fluid is to prepare the tube for the passage of the sperm and semen.

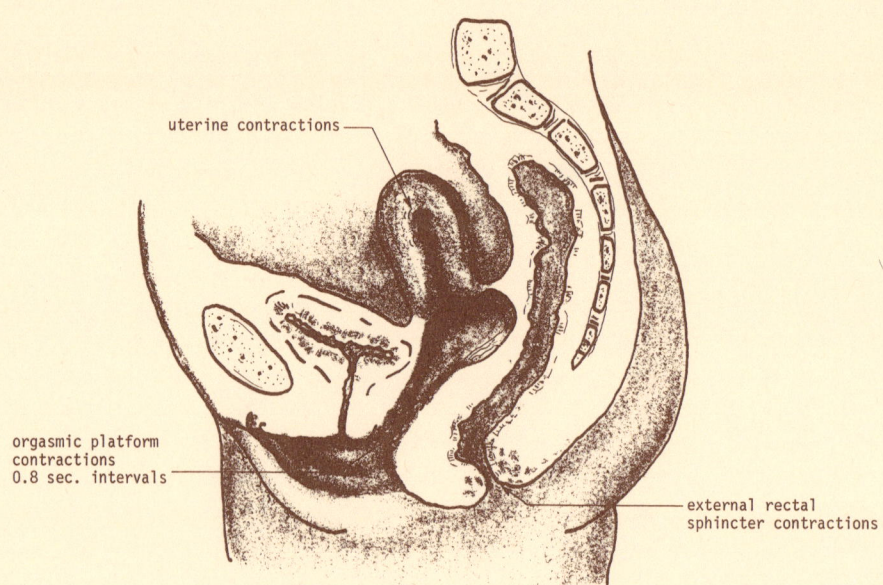

Female pelvis: orgasmic phase

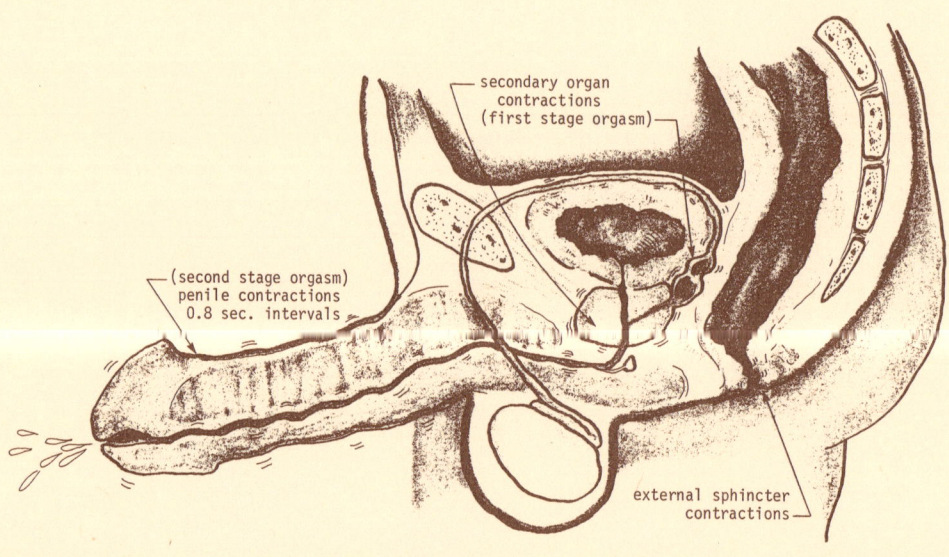

Male pelvis: orgasmic phase

PHASE III. ORGASM / BIOELECTRIC DISCHARGE

We come or climax. The tension is discharged suddenly, with great excitement and involuntary contractions of muscles, especially in the genital area. If ejaculation is to occur at all, it occurs now. Women do not ejaculate.

Female

The "orgasmic platform" has a noticeable spasm and a series of rhythmic contractions. The entire length of the vaginal barrel may ripple with contractions that begin in the farthest end of the uterus. The subjective experience of orgasm in women coincides with the first contraction of the outer third of the vagina or orgasmic platform. Effective stimulation needs to continue up to and through orgasm.

Male

Contractions in the man are differentiated into two stages. The first, which coincides with the experience of the "point of no return" is the contraction of the seminal vesicles and prostate gland. The semen is pushed out through the tube by the next wave of contractions.

The interval between the contractions is about eight-tenths seconds in both sexes.

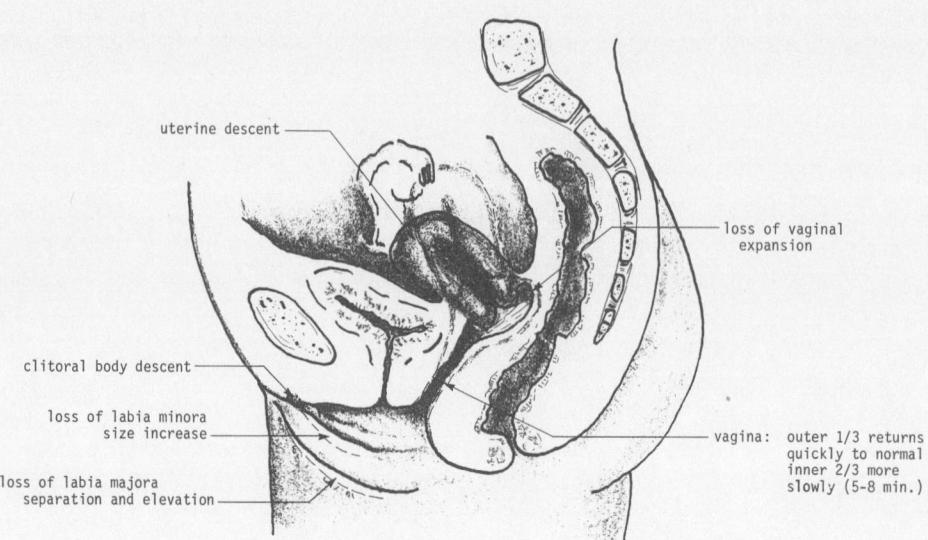

Female pelvis: resolution phase

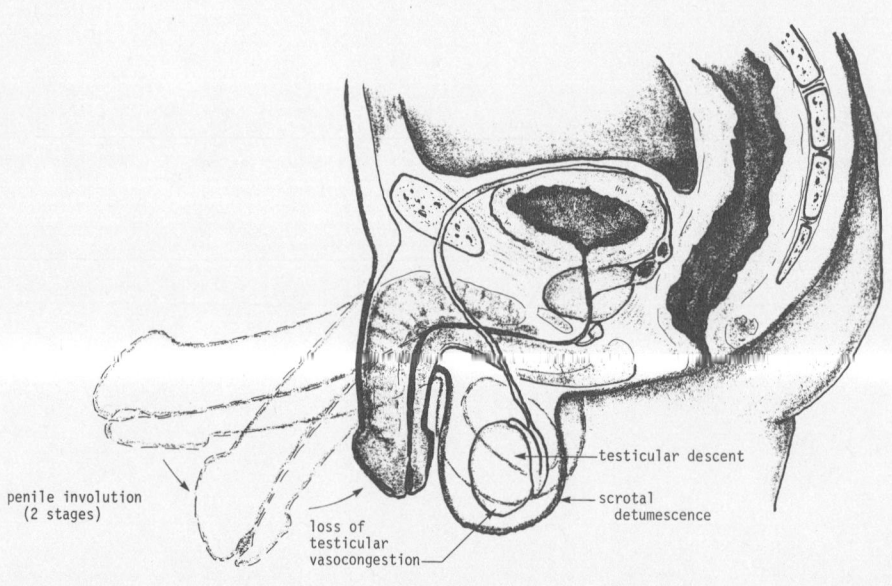

Male pelvis: resolution phase

sexual response

PHASE IV. RESOLUTION / MECHANICAL RELAXATION

The body now begins to return to its original pre-excitement state, a feeling of melting pleasure and calm. Sleep often occurs. Partners may feel especially tender and close. The expansion of orgasm is now integrated and appreciated.

PHASE V. REFRACTORY PERIOD / RESTING TIME

The time after orgasm in which little or no sexual excitement or charge is experienced, even if stimuli exist, is called the refractory period. According to the results of Johnson and Masters, it occurs primarily in men but there is evidence that it is also experienced by women. Some confusion results from the fact that many women are capable of experiencing multiple consecutive orgasms while relatively few males have this experience.

B

Draw a graph of your sexual response cycle each day this week. Try it again in a month.

Compare and contrast the experiences involved. Consider how they could be altered by better communication, feedback, or setting of the situation.

SEXUAL FANTASIES

Sexual fantasy can be thought of as a reorganization of bits and pieces of memory. These memories can be sensory, motor, or mental/symbolic. They may be so extensively reorganized that we don't even recognize the original components. Fantasies may contain the results of previous fantasies used in symbolic ways.

Some fantasies are very clear and well-defined. Others are merely fleeting impressions. Not all of our fantasies are sexual fantasies. They might be about the future, tonight's dinner, the next shopping trip, etc. Fantasies may occur in both waking or semi-sleep times, or they may occur during deep sleep; we usually call these last fantasies "dreams."

Fantasies may just happen spontaneously or we may try to conjure up fantasy material during sexual activity. Fantasy is most commonly used during masturbation.

Kinsey found that 64 percent of the women interviewed and 89 percent of the men fantasized while masturbating. So 36 percent of the women interviewed, and 11 percent of the men never fantasized while masturbating. People who fantasized while masturbating also sometimes fantasized while engaged in sexual activity with a partner. They also experienced some sexual dreaming.

As with other kinds of sexual activity, fantasy may be accompanied by any or all of the changes of the sexual response cycle.

For many people, fantasy seems to play an important role in their sexual motivation.

Fantasy can also be considered a sexual activity in its own right.

Fantasy may be a source of pleasure, but many of us have been erroneously taught that "normal" sex covers a very limited range of behavior. We sometimes feel guilty, embarrassed, or ashamed when our fantasies go beyond these limits. We should realize that both behavior and fantasy cover the whole range of sexual behavior in "normal" people. This is why it is useful to become aware of what other people do. We come to realize that our behavior and our fantasies are not "weird" or "far out." They are unique but widely shared.

Fantasy can be a useful tool in sexual enrichment. We may choose to enjoy our fantasies as they come to us or we may choose to act upon them in various ways. Talking over our sexual fantasies with others can give us a feeling of sharing and support and perhaps even generate more ideas to fantasize about. Sharing sexual fantasies with our sexual partner can be a powerfully intimate experience.

When we mutually decide to act on a particular fantasy, we may have a range of reactions and responses. Acting on a fantasy may increase or decrease its power as a fantasy or we may discover that the actuality is more or less satisfying than the fantasy.

If our fantasy is about a level or kind of experience that is difficult to obtain in "real" life, our attempts to act it out may prove disappointing. If we unconsciously turn our fantasy into an expectation we may devalue our current experience. Fantasizing about real possibilities while masturbating can be very helpful. By using deliberately structured fantasy during masturbation, for example, we may begin to feel more comfortable with new behaviors and attitudes.

Examining our fantasies carefully may give us useful information about ourselves. This is the method psychoanalysts and dream analysts use. Examining our fantasies also may give us an opportunity to reorganize and rearrange them to better suit current needs.

Fantasy is a wonderful and powerful tool with which we can examine and make changes in our sexuality. We will be working on fantasies in our at home exercises throughout this program.

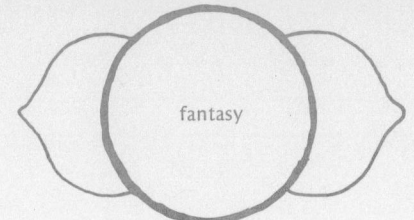

Fantasy Bibliography

Friday, Nancy. *My Secret Garden: Women's Sexual Fantasies.* New York: Trident Press, 1973. Paper, $1.50.
   A collection of women's fantasies compiled by Nancy Friday after she ran a series of newspaper ads requesting material for a study on women's fantasies. There is very little editorializing and lots of interesting information. The first real contribution about female fantasy since the Kinsey report.

Kronhausen, Phyllis and Eberhard Kronhausen. *Erotic Fantasies.* New York: Grove Press, 1969. Paper, $1.75.
   The Kronhausens believe that sexual fantasies are "safety-valves for bottled-up sex feelings, strivings, and wishes that are socially unacceptable," and in this book they review 500 years of Western erotic literature and folklore. They feel this book should provide a better understanding of human sex psychology than can be gained through clinical texts. For both professionals and non-professionals.

B

JOURNAL OF YOUR TURN-ONS

TURN-ONS

Underline every other word or phrase.

SMILEREDVELVETRICEMOUNDSSTAIRBANNISTERBLUESKYMANYCARSINSMALLALLEYTALLBUILDINGS WITHLONGROPESHOLDINGSCAFFOLDSBLUECOLUMNOF44SONTELEVISIONBUILDINGATTICBARNROUND FRUITCURVEOFFLANKTOFANNYLARGELIPSNECKEYESLARGEEYESBLUEEYESEARSBREASTSBIGTITS LARGEBREASTSLEGSBARELEGSBARELEGSINHEELSSLIMLEGSTHIGHSBLACKHOSEANKLEBRACELETFEET STARTOFANERECTIONHARDPENISTIGHTFITTINGPANTSBUMPSINPANTSHAIRLONGHAIRLONGBLONDE HAIRPETITFEATURESBEAUTIFULCOMPLEXIONSKINNYDIPPINGSHORTSKIRTSLOWNECKEDDRESSESSEE THRUBLOUSEJIGGLINGREARSSMALLGUYSBIGGUYSBRIGHTCOLORSREDCOLOREDLIGHTSLIGHTED CANDLESTILEFLOORSFUCKFILMSSOAPYBODIESHANDSHANDSTOUCHINGFINGERSMALEARMHAIRLESS MALEBODIESESPECIALLYARMSANDASSESHAIRHAIRYCHESTSFEETBAREFEETERECTIONSTARTOFAN ERECTIONNECKEARSEARLOBESBREASTSBIGTITSSOFTNIPPLESHARDNIPPLESTUMMYSCRATCHING SALIVAPELVICMOTIONBEINGNUDENUDEOUTOFDOORSTOUCHINGALLOVERSKINNYDIPPINGFIRMSOFT THINGSBABIESBABY'SBOTTOMLADY'STOUCHCUDDLINGNIBBLINGTICKLINGMERGINGDANCINGMASSAGES SUEDEVELVETSILKSHEETSFURRUGLEATHERWATERWARMWATERSHOWERWATERBEDSSLIPPERY KITTENFURRYTHINGSHORSEDOGKITTENGRASSCOOLBREEZEFOGMOISTCLAYRIPEPERSIMMONROUND FRUITKNEADINGBREADBREASTPIZZAMOVINGESCALATORHUGEPILLOWSVIBESFRESHLYBATHED PUSSYMOISTPUSSYBACKOFABABY'SNECKHAIRWHISKEYONBREATHSWEATPERFUMEMUSKINCENSE LIGHTEDCANDLESCOCKCAMPFIRESMOKEPIPETOBACCOSMOKEMARIJUANARAINROTTINGLEAVES PINECONESWOODSSPRINGMUDCOOLBREEZESSUEDEHALLWAYDOWNSTAIRSSWEETBASILSALTINESSOF SKINCHOCOLATEICECREAMPEPPERGUMBEINGFEDCOKEPIZZAMUSHROOMSLOXANYTHINGAFTERA LONGHIKERAINPEASOUPCUSTARDCHOCOLATEMALTFRESHAIRMOUNTAINWATERJUICEMOISTPUSSY RAINSEASOUNDSINFOGRAINDROPSSSOUNDOFORESTWATERPOUNDINGSURFBREATHINGSIGH LAUGHTERHAPPYPEOPLEDEEPTHROATEDCHUCKLEMUSICJIVESBELLSSWITCHEDONBACKTALKING CONVERSATIONWITHBOYFRIENDDOORTRAINSSEXGALSPELVICMOTIONBEINGOPENHAIRHOLDING BACKCOMINGTOGETHERBEINGONTOPLETTINGITALLHANGOUTSTRUGGLEFEARAGGRESSIVELOVE MAKINGPASSIONATEVIOLENCEMOTELSWALKINGTHRUDOORSGOODYPASTRYNOPANTIESTIGHT PANTSWITHNOPANTIES

MASTURBATION

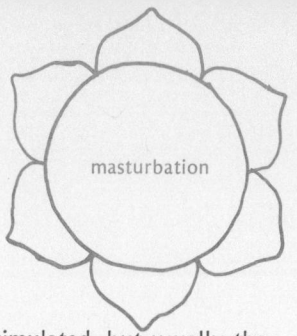

Masturbation is self-stimulation for sexual pleasure. All parts of the body may be stimulated, but usually the genitals are the focus. Masturbation usually leads to orgasm.

Masturbation is also known as:

Self-sexuality
Self-pleasuring
Auto-eroticism
Sex without a partner
Playing with yourself
Jacking off
Jilling off
Whacking off
Diddling, fiddling, twiddling / yourself
Onanism (incorrectly)

and negatively as "The hideous vice of self-pollution."

Masturbation Myths
1. Masturbation causes insanity, headaches, epilepsy, acne, blindness, nosebleeds, masturbator's heart, tenderness of the breasts, warts, nymphomania, undesirable odor, uninhibited sexuality, and hair on the palms.
2. Excessive masturbation is harmful.
3. It is an abnormal, unnatural act.
4. It is immature.
5. It is practiced mostly by simple-minded people.
6. It is a substitute for intercourse.
7. It is antisocial.
8. People may learn to prefer masturbation to intercourse.

Masturbation Truths
1. There is no evidence that masturbation impairs physical or mental health.
2. Masturbation is a natural function. People in most cultures and many species of animals masturbate.
3. Many people masturbate throughout their lives. Many sexually active people with available partners masturbate as an additional gratification.
4. Intercourse and masturbation can be viewed as complementary sexual experiences, not as mutually exclusive.
5. Masturbation is a good way to learn about your own sexual responses so you can communicate them to a partner.
6. Masturbation is a good way to create your own orgasm.

Masturbation is a natural sexual function. It is good psychologically and healthy physiologically.

The desire to masturbate occurs at different times for different people and the frequency varies enormously from person to person. Again, we are all different and unique. Some people fantasize while masturbating, others don't. Some people come quietly while masturbating, others make lots of sounds, and still others thrash about. These aspects vary greatly. There is no "right" or "best" way to masturbate or to have an orgasm.

It is natural for children to masturbate. Children masturbate out of curiosity and for pleasure. Guilt is a result of being told by OTHERS that it is wrong. The better informed and more comfortable we are about our own bodies and our own masturbation, the more clearly and effectively we can convey these values to our children.

Masturbation is not limited to genital jacking or jilling off but can include our whole bodies. Some people find ways to have orgasms without fondling their genitals manually, such as:

> Squeezing the legs together
> Kegel exercises
> Rubbing the pelvis against a pillow, bed, or the floor while on their stomach
> Running a stream of water over the genitals
> Fantasizing
> Caressing other places on the body: ears, nipples, thighs, etc.

There are other ways to have an orgasm: wearing tight pants, riding motorcycles, bicycles, or horses. Use your imagination.

Kinsey Data

Ninety percent of the men interviewed masturbated to orgasm in four minutes or less. Forty percent of women interviewed masturbated. Seventy percent of these women reached orgasm in 3 to 5 minutes. Of this 70 percent, masturbation was the most effective means of reaching orgasm for 95 percent. Masturbation is the surest, most frequent sexual activity in which orgasm takes place.

Reasons for Masturbation

> 1. Pure pleasure. It feels good.
> 2. To explore one's own response patterns.
> 3. To relieve sexual and other tensions.
> 4. To relieve pelvic congestion, especially during menstruation.
> 5. As reentry into sex after a heart attack or other medical ailments.
> 6. People who feel good about pleasuring themselves are much less likely to have sexual problems.
> 7. People who take responsibility for their sexual needs and responses seem to have good sexual adjustment.

Sharing masturbation experiences and developing sexual honesty with partners and friends is liberating for men and women.

Looking at your genitals as you masturbate (either directly or in a mirror or on video tape) breaks the taboos against looking at other people's genitals. Looking helps you to notice all the different parts as they really are. It will help you gain self-acceptance.

Masturbation in women helps keep the vaginal walls lubricated and stimulates secretions which keep the organs flexible and strong.

Masturbation can help in a relationship where there is a large difference in sexual taste or in the case of temporary changes in lifestyle (such as childbearing or separation). Masturbation takes the pressure off the partner to perform.

When men masturbate they stimulate the same genital areas—the balls, shaft, and head of the penis—that are

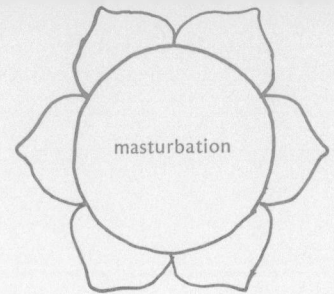

stimulated during intercourse. When women masturbate, the parts most often touched are the clitoral glans and shaft. These parts are often left unstimulated during penile-vaginal thrusting movements.

> If you don't use it, you lose it.
> An orgasm a day will keep you healthy and sane.
> Masturbate daily, if you like, or more often.
> Some persons masturbate more when they are having sex with partners.
> Our sexual interest varies over time and circumstance.
> It is okay to use a dildo when masturbating. Many women and men enjoy something penetrating them in vagina or anus while they masturbate.
> Use fingers or dildoes, but be careful not to hurt yourself.

A vibrator can be appreciated more if seen as a sex aid, not a sexual competitor. For more orgasms and intense sexual pleasure, a vibrator is a valuable aid for many people. Vibrators come in many sizes, styles and intensities. They can enhance sexual pleasure for you—alone or with your partner.

Masturbation can be your primary sexual outlet if you choose.

Even though you have had sexual partners, your first orgasm may happen while masturbating.

We can learn to expand our range of masturbation practices—with sounds, smells, oils, lotions, pictures, books, photos, films, partners, groups, whatever pleases.

Only you can learn whether you like to:

> Sweat
> Gasp
> Groan
> Tighten your jaw, your toes
> Curl your tongue, your toes
> Suck your knuckle, your toes
> Breathe heavily
> Feel good
> Be alone
> Be with another person(s) . . . or something else, or not.

You can give yourself the choice of masturbating to orgasm, or not.

Masturbation Bibliography

Dodson, Betty. *Liberating Masturbation.* San Francisco: 1974. Paper, $3.50. A timely and exciting book about masturbation as a sexual base. Ms. Dodson describes her own life struggles and awareness of her sexuality, her body, her art, and her body-sex workshops. The many drawings of female genitals begin the new positive esthetic of the beauty of each woman's uniqueness. Also describes helpful hints on loving your body through yoga, food, and lifestyle.

Gordon, David. *Self-Love.* Baltimore: Penguin, 1972. Paper, $1.00. Gordon's purpose is to explore the subject of masturbation and help people understand its normalcy. He first gives the facts, then shows how far back the guilt tradition goes. He then explores humanity's desire for unity in life and relates this desire to sexuality.

Smith, Carolyn, Toni Ayres, and Maggi Rubenstein. *Getting in Touch: Self Sexuality for Women.* Photos by Laird Sutton. San Francisco: Multi Media Resource Center, 1973. Paper, $1.95. By women for women, this book is about getting in touch with the body and learning how it feels. Some specific ideas on how to begin exploring one's self-sexuality are given. The photographs show women doing the body and genital explorations. The Kegel exercises are included.

SENSATE FOCUS

Sensate focus is a popular phrase now. It means paying total attention to specific sensory or tactile stimulation. We may broaden this term to include any input to our senses, such as temperature, taste, smell, etc.

Touch is as necessary as breathing to the well-being of the whole body. Our skin is the most extensive organ of our bodies. Orgasm occurs principally through effective stimulation of various skin areas. Most of us have received little instruction in the art of touching. A little learning about touching very often results in a great increase in the pleasure experienced in sexual activity.

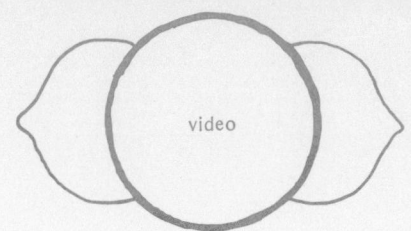

VIDEO – WEEK 1.

VIDEO DESCRIPTIONS – WHAT TO LOOK FOR

"UNFOLDING" explores the world of fantasy and the multiple images there. It is a search for fantasy fulfillment through memory re-organization and image transformation. Look for fantasy archetypes—images and patterns common to most people's fantasy and mythic worlds throughout history. Ask yourself, How many different kinds of sexual behavior are there?

"SHIRLEY" takes a gradual approach to the total body. The film fully explores the strokes and touches of self-pleasuring, emphasizing the total body, hair, skin, neck, use of a vibrator, and even sex flush on feet.

"MARGO" Look for the orgasmic ripples after the first sharp spasm, distinct changes in the breasts, the film of sweat over entire body. Margo looks at her own genitals in the mirror, strokes face and breast; and clitoris and vagina simultaneously.

"FEELING GOOD" presents masturbation as one of the most positive sex acts for a man. Emphasizes the importance of choosing a pleasurable context for the experience and the many different types of sensual experiences to be had, including anal exploration.

AT HOME EXERCISE PROGRESSION

	Section B Page No.

With Yourself:

7. Look at Two Different Kinds of Erotic Literature — 65
8. Imagine That — 65
9. Genital Exam — 66
10. Whole Body Masturbation — 67
11. Masturbation with Teasing, Tasting and Smelling — 68

With Your Partner:

12. Talking and Listening — 68
13. Masturbation Experience — 69

Repeat Exercises:

Repeat Breathing Exercises—2a, 2c, 2d, 2i
Repeat Sensory Awareness Exercise—3a, 3b
Repeat Kegels—Exercise 4

Remember your journal.

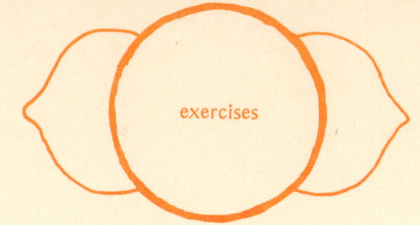

AT HOME EXERCISE 7—LOOK AT TWO DIFFERENT KINDS OF EROTIC LITERATURE

Many people find that reading erotic literature or "pornography" has a whole range of effects on them. Looking or reading can be an aphrodisiac, a mood-shifter or a fantasy-starter. Other reactions are: interest, curiosity, neutrality, anger, turn-off, disgust, etc.

There is a wide variety of erotic and "pornographic" literature available. Some can be found at your local bookstore or "adult" bookstore. Glance through some of these and select two different kinds of materials for yourself. When you have completed this exercise, write about your feelings and reactions going to the store to look at or buy your erotica.

B

AT HOME EXERCISE 8—MAKE UP A NEW FANTASY

Imagine that:

Time guide—10 minutes

65

AT HOME EXERCISE 9—GENITAL EXAM

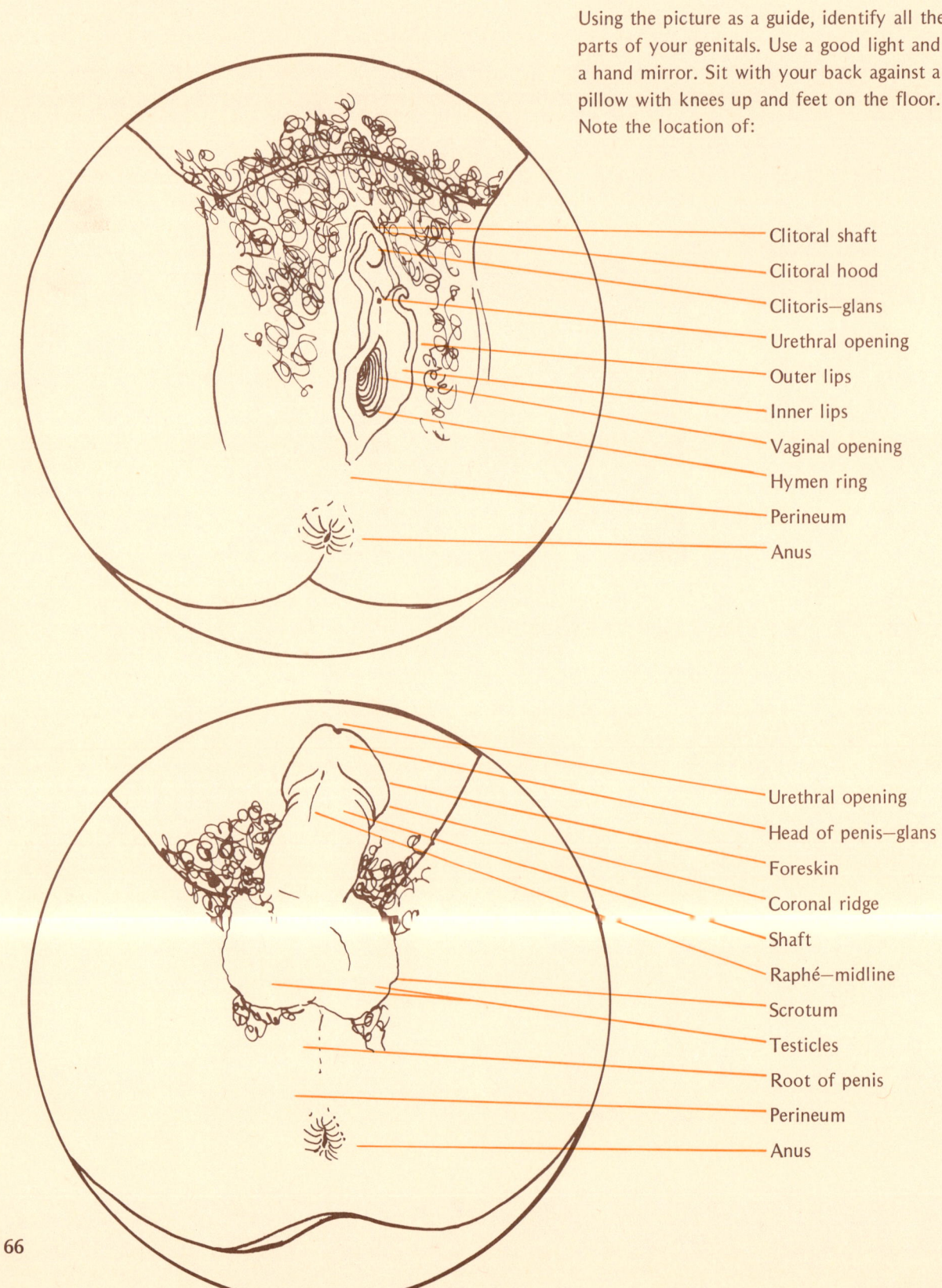

Using the picture as a guide, identify all the parts of your genitals. Use a good light and a hand mirror. Sit with your back against a pillow with knees up and feet on the floor. Note the location of:

- Clitoral shaft
- Clitoral hood
- Clitoris—glans
- Urethral opening
- Outer lips
- Inner lips
- Vaginal opening
- Hymen ring
- Perineum
- Anus

- Urethral opening
- Head of penis—glans
- Foreskin
- Coronal ridge
- Shaft
- Raphé—midline
- Scrotum
- Testicles
- Root of penis
- Perineum
- Anus

exercises

Note the texture and color of the skin of each part. Move the hood of the clitoris back and forth over the glans. Move the foreskin back and forth over the head of the penis.

See that it moves easily back and forth. If it feels painful, check it out with your doctor or local clinic right away. If your doctor doesn't seem to care about the problem, find one who does. Using a finger, begin to stroke lightly different parts of your genitals to see which strokes feel best and which places feel best. If the area feels too dry, try some bland oil, lotion, saliva, vaginal juice, etc. Place two fingers into the outer third of the vagina and tighten the P.C. muscle around them. Try to suck your fingers into the vagina by pulling up, and then try to force them out by bearing down. See how much strength these muscles have. Have you thought about giving a name to your genitals?

B

AT HOME EXERCISE 10 — WHOLE-BODY MASTURBATION

This exercise will incorporate different parts of the body into masturbation.

While you are spending your hour stimulating yourself, think of other parts of your body that might feel good to touch. Some examples:

>Breasts
>Face
>Inside of arms
>Inside of legs
>Stomach, neck, shoulders, thighs, feet, chest.

Use both hands, one on your genitals and the other somewhere else, at the same time. Close your eyes and try to get in touch with stroking both places simultaneously. As you do this breathe slowly and evenly. Imagine the breath flowing along a path between the two places you are touching and stroking. See if this helps expand your sexual experience. Don't forget your anus, and relax . . . explore. (Don't put anything in your vagina that has been in your anus.)

AT HOME EXERCISE 11 — MASTURBATION WITH TEASING, SMELLING, AND TASTING

Do this for approximately one hour.

This exercise will assist you in learning how your body feels at the different stages of the sexual response cycle. Learn to build up sexual pleasure, then let it subside, become aware of the feelings, relax a little, and then continue. This is known as TEASING.

Masturbate until you feel your breathing increase,
> until you feel like going very fast,
> until you experience wanting to thrust your pelvis.

Then stop and experience these feelings for awhile.

Do not aim for an orgasm.

Take a short break, one or two minutes.

Now begin again to stimulate yourself, using light stroking. Incorporate the Kegels you have learned. When there is sufficient lubrication in your vagina, or when you notice a secretion from the penis, take a few moments to smell and taste your secretions. It is okay to taste your own secretions. If you didn't have these secretions, your vagina or urethra would become dry and cracked. If you and your partner have experienced oral sex you might compare notes on your perception of the tasting and smelling experience. Was there any difference between your reactions to smelling and tasting?

After you have teased yourself two to three times you may wish to rest, go on, or do whatever you wish.

AT HOME EXERCISE 12 — TALKING AND LISTENING (PARTNER)

Often there are times when we do not express our real feelings to our partners because we don't know how our partners will react, or we are afraid of how they will or won't react. If is often especially difficult to convey negative feelings.

The purpose of this exercise is to provide each of you an open "safe" space in which to express your feelings about something, and to provide the assurance that you have been heard.

Ask your partner to read the rules of this communication exercise. Arrange with your partner to set aside a twenty-minute period in which to do this exercise.

Decide who will be the talker (A) first. The talker (A) talks for about five minutes about something that she/he has feelings about, using statements beginning with "I" such as "*I* want," "*I* feel," "*I* did," "*I* am," as much as possible and avoiding statements like "*you* always," "*you* want," etc. The listener (B) *may not* interrupt except to ask for clarification—for example: "Could you be more specific? " When the talker (A) is finished, the listener (B) says "thank you" (for sharing that information).

Then the second talker (B) begins to talk for five minutes. The listener (A) may not interrupt. If the second talker (B) wishes to make a comment about what A said during those five minutes, that's okay as long as the talker sticks to his/her *own* feelings on the subject.

A says "thank you" when B is finished.

Many people find it helpful to wait at least twenty-four hours before responding with anything other than "thank you."

After the first round, don't talk about that subject for a couple of hours . . . or . . . negotiate for another subject. Some of your negotiation with your partner can include deciding whether to take on a non-sexual or a sexual topic.

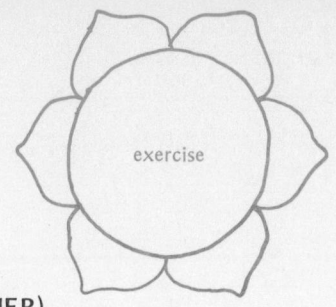

AT HOME EXERCISE 13 — MASTURBATION EXPERIENCE (SELF OR PARTNER)

The questions listed below will serve as a guide in sharing information with your partner and will help clarify your own views and attitudes.

Arrange to have at least an hour when you will not be interrupted. You may proceed by having each partner ask the other Question 1. When both have answered, go on to Question 2, and so on. Or one partner may ask all the questions of the other, then switch. When your partner has answered each question, acknowledge that you have understood and say thank you.

If you don't have a partner now, you can do this with a consenting friend, of either sex, or with yourself in front of a mirror, or in your journal.

1. What is the earliest self-pleasuring you can remember?
2. When did you first associate self-pleasuring with masturbation?
3. How did you learn to masturbate? (self-discovery, friend, etc.)
4. When did you have your first conversation about masturbation?
5. How did you feel about masturbation as a teenager?
6. How do you feel about masturbation now?
7. What is your current pattern? How do you do it and how do you feel about it?

Journal Reminder

Feelings and Reactions to:
　At home exercises, video, discussion

Feelings and reactions about:
　Fantasies, masturbation, sharing with your partner

For next week read about:　　　　　Section C
　　　　　　　　　　　　　　　　　　　Page No.

　Male Sexuality　　　　　　　　　　　72
　Male Homosexuality　　　　　　　　74
　Desensitization and Sexual Patterns　77
　Female Sexuality　　　　　　　　　　81
　Lesbianism　　　　　　　　　　　　　88
　Bisexuality　　　　　　　　　　　　　91
　Celibacy　　　　　　　　　　　　　　94

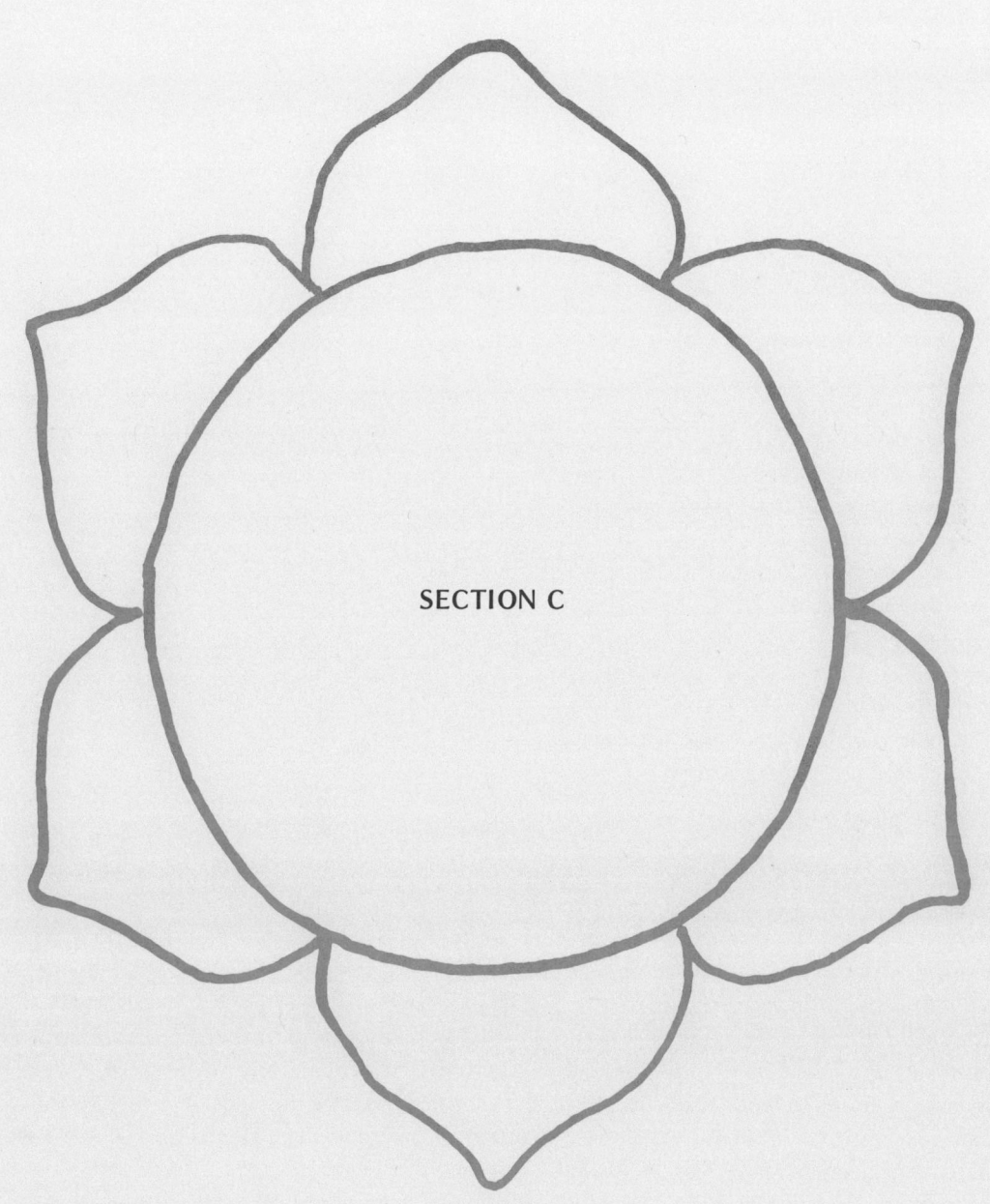

MALE SEXUALITY

MYTHS AND SOCIETAL MESSAGES

Do: perform.
get it up.
achieve.
keep it up.
initiate.
work.
always be turned on.
be young.
be a sex machine.
protect.
measure up.
control.
be responsible.
fuck only young attractive women.
know what to do.
give women orgasms.
have a big cock.
succeed.
score.
rationalize.
hide your feelings of fear, inadequacy, rejection or helplessness.
keep a stiff upper lip.

Don't: quit.
fail.
enjoy yourself.
play.
feel.
be vulnerable, weak, receptive, or gay.
take strokes.
be honest about your real sexual needs, especially with women.
be passive.
let go.
take responsibility for birth control.

Men are taught to rigidly conform to these cultural myths and have lots of guilt and negative feelings if they don't hold up their end, especially if their sexual needs differ from the culturally-accepted norms. If they have difficulty in achieving the standards of maleness they are told to remain silent and bear the load. The limits imposed by these standards inhibit men from exploring and fulfilling the total range of sexual options. Most men have great difficulty in finding social support in making changes to suit their personal needs and desires.

To achieve a full and satisfying sex life, men need what women need: self-knowledge, facts, options, techniques, and honesty. Read the section on female sexuality.

Many men are not even conscious of the possibility that things can be different, that the process of altering and examining the old roles and myths can have an effect on their own lives. Men often feel depressed and hopeless about changing anything. We fear the loss of our power.

Men usually get their sex education and information in situations where competition, performance, and accomplishment are matters of status. Locker-room bragging is a common example. As men, we have been taught to perform, compete, work, and initiate sex. As a result, a large part of our personhood gets left out of our lives. Our sexuality is limited by the old myths.

Talking with other men as friends rather than as competitors can help us find out what men really do and how we feel about what we do.

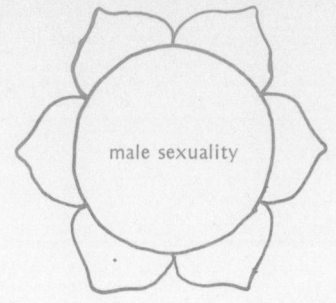
male sexuality

INCREASE YOUR OPTIONS

1. Receive strokes. Explain to your partner how you want to be touched.
2. Share feelings. Ask your partner to share with you.
3. Masturbate freely; be your own lover at least one day a week.
4. Have sex only when you want it.
5. Seek the kinds of sexual experiences you want.
6. Learn to play with your sexual response cycle. Imagine how you would like something you've never tried.
7. Fantasize while you masturbate.
8. Find some fantasy you can act on alone, and do it.
9. Find a willing partner and act on some of your fantasies.
10. Say yes when you want to.
11. Say no when you want to.
12. Learn about your body and what you like.
13. Talk about sex with your partner.
14. Take care of your body.
15. Pamper yourself.
16. Touch yourself all over.
17. Take a long hot bath for pleasure after you shower for cleanliness.
18. Stroke your body with velvet, feathers, leather, anything you wish.
19. Touch your partner's body for *your* own pleasure.
20. Ask your partner for one thing you want done.
21. Have a sexual experience with your partner *without* having coitus.
22. Lick.
23. Breathe.
24. Look at your body, all over, in a mirror.
25. Look at your partner's body.
26. Don't perform. Note that the world (and the affair) doesn't come to an end.

(See also the section on Masturbation.)

Suggested Books on Male Sexuality

Feigen-Fasteau, Marc. *The Male Machine.* New York: McGraw-Hill, 1974. Cloth, $7.95. This is a personal account of the destructive effects of the American male stereotype on himself and the rest of the male population. Feigen-Fasteau opens up the myths and projects an optimistic future of androgyny when paralyzing sex roles fall away.

McIlvenna, Ted. *When You Don't Make It.* Photos by Laird Sutton. San Francisco: Multi Media Resource Center, 1973. Paper, $1.95. In the *YES Book of Sex* series. This is a book for men who are experiencing secondary impotence. The book offers reassurance that it is a normal occasional occurrence, and talks about getting in touch with the body. The techniques described can also be used to make masturbation more pleasurable.

McIlvenna, Ted, and Herb Vandervoort, M.D. *You Can Last Longer.* Photos by Laird Sutton. San Francisco: Multi Media Resource Center, 1973. Paper, $1.95. In the *YES Book of Sex* series, *You Can Last Longer* gives the behavioral method of treating premature ejaculation, known as the Seamans squeeze technique. The photographs show a couple moving through the process step-by-step.

HOMOSEXUALITY

Homosexuality is one of the most harshly condemned states of being in our traditionally anti-sexual Judeo-Christian culture. And because our society is male-oriented, most of the concern about homosexuality has been directed toward the male homosexual. That is, until very recently most of the research in this area has focused on male homosexuality, and most homosexuals who run into trouble with the law are men. Nevertheless, social pressure and harassment do not seem to have much effect on the incidence of male homosexuality. This lifestyle has been with us throughout recorded history and will undoubtedly continue to be the preference of a certain percentage of men.

Alfred Kinsey and his colleagues, in their precedent-shattering book *Sexual Behavior in the Human Male* published in 1948, found that 37 percent of American males have at least one homosexual experience to orgasm after the age of puberty, while another 13 percent have homosexual urges but do not act on them. That adds up to 50 percent. The Kinsey statistics indicate that, in any given three-year period, 30 percent of the males in this country have incidental homosexual experience, 25 percent have more than incidental homosexual experience, 18 percent have as much homosexual as heterosexual experience, 10 percent are more or less exclusively homosexual, and 8 percent are exclusively homosexual. Four percent of the men in this country, their findings showed, are exclusively homosexual throughout their lives.

The Kinsey figures are twenty-seven years old. Current indications are that homosexual activity between men is far more widespread in 1975 than it appeared to be in 1948. Despite this information, however, and despite the gains made by the gay liberation movement in educating the society at large, male homosexuality is still looked upon as a taboo activity. Here are some of the myths that continue to obscure the truth:

Myth: All male homosexuals are effeminate.

Fact: Male homosexuals are a cross-section of all men. They come from every part of our society and they work in every kind of job. It is true that some gay men fit the stereotype of the effeminate man—but so do some heterosexual men. Some gay men accent their "feminine" characteristics either for the fun of it or to flaunt their gayness to a hostile society. But most gay men are indistinguishable from all other men.

Myth: Male homosexuals are child molesters and prey on youth.

Fact: Most sexual assaults on children are heterosexual (97 percent) and occur within the family context, that is, they are commited by fathers, stepfathers, uncles, brothers, close friends. In a survey made in San Francisco in 1972 there were 107 reported incidences of child molesting. All were by heterosexuals. Most homosexuals seek lovers and friends from their own peer/age group. Some, however, fall prey to the American cult of youth and seek companions younger than themselves.

homosexuality

Myth: Male homosexuals are sexually promiscuous.

Fact: Alfred Kinsey once defined a promiscuous person as someone who is getting more than you are. Many gay men experience sexual contacts with many different partners. This is true partly because they are thrust into a sexual subculture. The gay man is not free to approach other men unless he knows they are gay for fear of being found out and thus losing his job and/or friends. Gathering places such as bars and steam baths are safe places to make sexual contacts but difficult places to make friendships. Many gay men have long-term relationships with one partner; many such relationships allow for outside sexual activity by both. Others prefer to live singly or in communal situations. Some are celibate.

Myth: The kind of sex two men have is perverted.

Fact: The sexual activity between two men is very much like the sexual activity between two women or a woman and man. As with other human beings, men express their sexual feelings for each other in a variety of ways, such as touching, fondling, kissing, and pleasuring. Mutual masturbation, oral-genital stimulation, and anal-genital intercourse are common means of sexual fulfillment.

Myth: When two homosexuals form a partnership one plays the woman's role and the other plays the man's.

Fact: Male homosexuals are men who prefer other men. Therefore, when they live together they are living together as men. Admittedly, some couples do imitate heterosexual "marriage," that being the only model they have known. Generally these men outgrow role-playing and eventually establish a relationship based on their own needs and personalities.

Myth: Male homosexual relationships never last.

Fact: Gay relationships between men appear to be more difficult to maintain than those between women. This has more to do with societal attitudes than anything else. It is considered all right for a man to remain a bachelor, but as Dr. Martin Hoffman pointed out in his book *Gay World*, our society looks askance at two men living together (especially after the age of thirty). Pressures of job, society, and parents often put unbearable strains on such a relationship. Despite such pressures, however, many male homosexuals do form lasting relationships.

Myth:	Male homosexuals are woman-haters.	Fact:	The majority of gay men don't hate women; they prefer men. However, male homosexuals are raised with the same concepts of women as are male heterosexuals. As Ingrid Bengis has said so well in her book *Combat in the Erogenous Zone*, there is a bit of woman-hating in all men and a bit of man-hating in all women. Male chauvinism is not restricted to straight men; gay men suffer from this social disease too. Many gay men are married to women. They marry for many reasons: job security, fear of growing old alone, societal pressure, the desire for children, the desire to hide their homosexuality from others. Far too many counselors of all professions are still suggesting to young gay men that all they need do is get married and the "phase" will pass. This is not true, and this mistaken advice leads to many unhappy marriages.

The status of homosexuality has gone through many changes over the centuries. It was originally considered a sin, then a crime. Now it is thought by most to be a "sickness." Hopefully this concept is on its way out. In 1974 the American Psychiatric Association voted to remove homosexuality from the list of mental illnesses in its Standard Diagnostic Manual. It will be some time before everyone agrees with this decision, but it is a step forward. Eventually, perhaps, homosexuality will truly be seen for what it is—one variation on the total spectrum of human sexuality.

The following books should be helpful for additional insight into male homosexuality.

Fisher, Peter. *The Gay Mystique: The Myth and Reality of Male Homosexuality.* New York: Stein & Day, 1972. Paper, $1.95. An excellent overview of male homosexuality by a gay man. Explores the myths, fears, and unknowns. Describes the arguments for and against homosexuality.

Gearhart, Sally and William R. Johnson. *Loving Women/Loving Men: Gay Liberation and the Church.* San Francisco: Glide Publications, 1974. Paper, $6.95. A powerful look at religious persecution of gay women and men. Discusses the Sodom and Gomorrah myth and how the church is currently relating to gay people. Strong section on how gay women and men feel about the church.

Lee, Ronald D., Frank Melleno, and Robert Mullis. *Gay Men Speak.* San Francisco: Multi Media Resource Center, 1973. Paper, $1.95. Photographs. A statement on how gay men feel about love, relationships, sex and life. A good beginning in forming positive attitudes. This is a part of the *YES Book of Sex* series.

Weinberg, George. *Society and the Healthy Homosexual.* New York: Doubleday, 1973. Paper, $1.95. Weinberg describes homophobia, the hatred and fear of homosexuality, and how to overcome this prejudice. One chapter of this excellent book is on communication with parents.

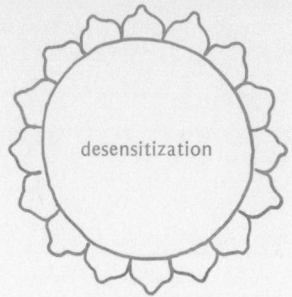

DESENSITIZATION

Of all the words in the English language, (there are about four hundred thousand in common use) there are seven words prohibited from use on television. These words: Piss, Shit, Fuck, Cunt, Cocksucker, Motherfucker, and Tits, are banned (in 1975) from use in any way. Comedians like Lenny Bruce and George Carlin have made attempts to bring this to the attention of their audiences and have been dubbed sick or dirty comics as a result. The fact is that these so-called dirty words are the very words most of us actually use when we try to describe sexual behaviors. The same prohibition exists regarding visual images. These words and images have a negative "charge" and people feel that as a shock whenever they hear them in public. The forbidden words and images are often replaced with medical or abstract terms in an effort to give people information without "appealing to prurient interests."

The purpose of desensitization (or demythologizing) in the SAR process is to reduce that negative "charge" so that people can use these words freely if they wish when talking about sexual acts in a casual and non-judgmental way. This is what is meant by the idea expressed in the National Sex Forum Assumptions that people have a right to a "realistic objectification of the range of behavior," in other words, what people actually do, how they describe it and how they feel about it.

One of the most effective ways of reducing the negative charge on a word or image is through repetition in a neutral context. Actually you have already been doing that from the beginning of this program with the images of sexual behavior presented in the SAR videotapes.

On the following pages you will find some words that are generally considered to have the connotation of "dirty" words. These games or exercises are designed to help you to reduce the negative charge on the verbal level. This is also true of the SAR videotape *Titles Available.* While viewing this tape, the words that are being flashed on the screen along with those being spoken can aid in your desensitization. Say the words to yourself along with Bill, either aloud or silently.

The next step in desensitization is the set of SAR videotapes in the Sexual Patterns series. These images are provided to give you a sense of the range of behavior people engage in—the differences and the samenesses. The patterns of each individual and couple are uniquely their own, and are not to be taken as ideal or correct. The people in these tapes are different from each other in many ways even though the sexual acts may be similar. Our own sexual patterns are probably the most unique thing about us. While viewing these tapes see if you can notice how many different activities are being shown, how the actions are linked together by the people as they go through the sexual response cycle, and how they relate and share their feelings about themselves with each other. After viewing this set of tapes, you might wish to compare these sexual patterns with your own or with others you have read about or seen.

If you are interested in exploring this further, try a pornographic movie or book with the intention of observing the sexual patterns of the people. Compare what you see in these images with your own personal history and with your fantasies.

Remember, there is no right way or wrong way to express your sexuality, only your way.

The Range of Behavior—What People Do

On the one hand, men and women share

> mouth
> tongue
> face
> lips
> nipples
> hands
> fingers
> belly
> nose
> back
> head
> anus
> ass
> feet
> legs
> toes

And, on the other hand, we have differences:

> cock
> prick
> hard-on
> penis
> lingam
> rod
> peter
> cunt
> vagina
> yoni
> jade chamber
> womb
> pussy
> tits
> breast
> knockers
> boobs
> clitoris
> little man in the boat
> prostate
> balls
> testicles

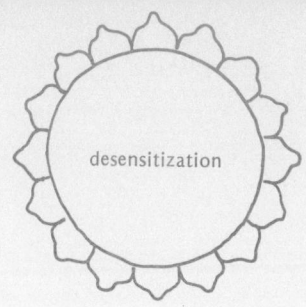

desensitization

These can all be put to erotic use in endless combination:

fucking (cock in cunt, cock in anus)
screwing
balling
cocksucking
cuntlicking
cuntlapping
clitlicking
clitrubbing
finger fucking
stroking, jerking or jilling off
nuzzling
massage
fist fucking
asshole screwing
analingus
69
sodomy
fellatio
cunnilingus
coitus
intercourse
digital
manual
petting
necking
going down on
getting into
masturbation
menage a trois
orgy

Draw a line between all the words that mean the same.

straight	slang	peter	hard-on	
prick	cunt	redhead	boobs	
lovelips	anus	penis	slit	jade chamber
vagina	lingam	knockers	breast	phallus
pussy	throbbing engine	testicles	schmuck	gism
clitoris	clit	shot his wad	balling	stick
masturbation	little man in the boat	fucking	coitus	sodomy
screwing	cornholed	fellatio	hairy cave	love box
cunnilingus	cocksucking	nuts	orgasm	intercourse
cuntlicking	family jewels	yoni	going down on	petting
raincoat	balls	rubber	jerking off	ejaculation
necking	love juice	semen	asshole screwing	deep throat
analingus	getting in to	condom	rimming	jilling off
stroking	asshole	nuzzle	tits	juicy
come	rod	coming	rod	climax
fist fucking	sixtynine	cunt	cock	finger fucking

FEMALE SEXUALITY

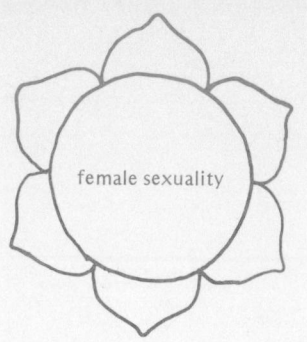

    EARLY MESSAGES
    SOCIETAL MESSAGES
        GUILT   CONFUSION   DEPENDENCY   FEAR   ALONENESS

These things are our heritage.

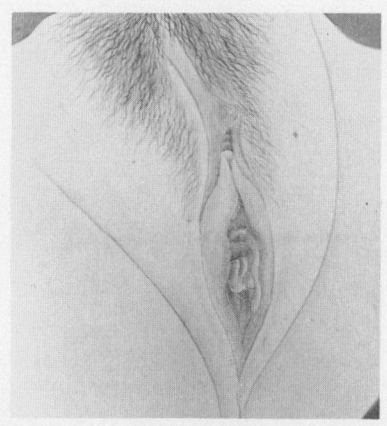 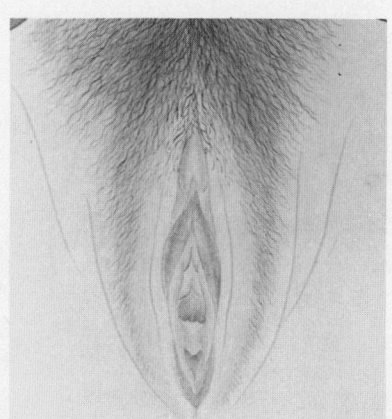 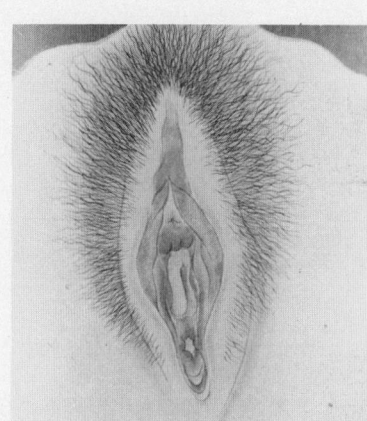

C

We can overcome through

    SELF-KNOWLEDGE
    FACTS
    OPTIONS
    TECHNIQUES
    HONESTY
    SHARING

EARLY MESSAGES

Don't: touch "down there."
talk about sex.
learn about sex.
read about sex.
think about or experiment with sex.
get turned on.
get out of control.
let your partner get out of control.
give in to sexual desire.
be available.
look at your genitals.
let anyone else look at your genitals.
kiss on the first date.
feel sexual.
get a "bad" reputation.
be too forward.
play doctor.

Do: be attractive, obedient, passive.
maintain a "good reputation."
wait for the male to initiate.
use sex for non-sexual reasons.
expect the man to know all about sex.
refuse a man when he asks you to be sexual.

SOCIETAL MESSAGES

Sex is only for men's pleasure and to produce babies.
You *should* only have sex if you're married.
You *should* only have sex with men.
You *should* save that valuable "thing" for your husband (a certain part of your anatomy).
You *must* marry . . . a man.
You *should* please your man.
You *should* deodorize your genitals.
You *should* only share love with one person.
Only a man can touch your genitals.
Sex is dirty; sexual urges are bad.
Anything other than the "missionary position" is dirty.
You *should not* have sex during your period.
Don't seem too experienced (even if you are).
If your orgasm doesn't happen, *fake it.*
Your naked body is shameful.
Your body will never measure up to the perfect commercial norm.
Women shouldn't be too successful, even sexually.
You won't get a man if you are "tarnished."
Sex is for male pleasure; fill his needs, not your own . . . it's your obligation (duty).

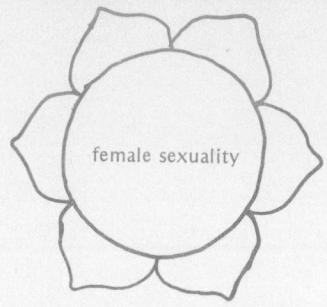

female sexuality

You must have a "vaginal" orgasm. (Freud said that there are two kinds of women's orgasm: clitoral orgasm from clitoral stimulation, which is immature; and vaginal orgasm from penile thrusting, the "right" mature kind.)
You *must* have an orgasm.
Women don't ever have orgasms.
If you want clitoral stimulation you are: too demanding, immature, selfish.
You *must* have orgasms in missionary position.
It takes too long to turn women on.
Foreplay is a questionable practice because intercourse is the goal of sex.
You *shouldn't* touch yourself during sex.
You *should* have sex on your back.
All your pleasure *should* come from the movements of the man's cock.
You *must* have a perfect figure.
Birth control is the woman's job.
You *must* have sex on demand.
You *must* have sex every night.
You *must* come when the man does.
Sex is better left a mystery.
You need a man to be complete.
You *must* be free and groovy while figuring all this out.
Only doctors and men know how a woman's body works.

CAN ALL OF THIS BE TRUE?

If our genitals are so valuable, why does everyone talk about them as if they were dirty?
If sex is so beautiful, why does everyone talk as if it was so dirty?
If sex is prohibited before marriage, how can you be expected to perform perfectly after you get married?
Etc., etc., etc.?

HOW TO GET OUT OF IT

It's no wonder that we as women are often

         confused and men are confused.
         objectified, guilty, alone, and worried.
         uncomfortable with our own bodies.
         expecting men to know everything.
         faking orgasm.
         turning off.
         waiting for *it* to happen to us.
         masturbating in secret, if at all.
         embarrassed about our genitals.
         worried about how our genitals smell and taste.
and
         so many of us haven't had orgasms yet.

BECOMING A POSITIVE SEXUAL PERSON

Women are becoming more interested in learning about their own sexuality. Up to this time, our lack of information about ourselves and our bodies, and the implied secrecy surrounding female sexuality have kept us from talking frankly to one another and to our partners.

WE NEED SELF-KNOWLEDGE, FACTS, OPTIONS, TECHNIQUES, HONESTY.

SELF-KNOWLEDGE

Self-knowledge is attainable through work and the sharing of information.

1. Learn as much about your own body as possible. Learn how to keep it healthy (this includes genital hygiene, relaxation, body awareness and exercises, food).
2. Read, explore, examine your feelings.
3. Begin talking with other women about what being sexual and being a woman really is for you (not how you think society *expects* you to act and feel, but how you honestly feel). Find out how they feel.
4. Examine your genitals with a mirror. Get to know them; they are yours and they are beautiful.
5. Learn about your own sexual responses, fantasies, turn-ons, preferences.
6. Have a frank discussion with your partner about who initiates sex.
7. State your pleasures positively. (For example, saying "I'm turned on by clitoral stimulation" is much better than saying "I need clitoral stimulation.")
8. Devote time alone to taking care of yourself.
9. Try new things.
10. Remember, you can control your sexual definition of yourself. You can choose any option, change your mind, and do whatever you like.
11. Determine your sexual needs and how you can best meet them.
12. Read about sex; find the words to express yourself.

FACTS

1. The clitoris is our primary sex organ.
2. There are as many nerve endings in the clitoris (glans, shaft, hood) as there are in the penis.
3. There are far fewer nerve endings in the vagina. Most sensitivity is in the outer third of the vagina, although there are pressure receptors in the back two-thirds.
4. Over half of women DO NOT have orgasms with penile-vaginal thrusting alone.
5. Most women reach orgasm during intercourse through clitoral stimulation (by themselves, by their partners, or with a vibrator).
6. Kinsey said: Women can and do enjoy sex as much as men. Women are not frigid; both men and women lack information about female sexuality. Women are orgasm-seeking creatures (just as men are).
7. Masters and Johnson said: There is no difference between a "vaginal" and a "clitoral" orgasm. The orgasm happens the same way no matter what kind of stimulation is used (manual, oral, coital, fantasy, breast stimulation, or vibrator). Women are capable of multiple orgasms (from two to over 50), but some prefer to have only one or a few. Women's orgasms vary in intensity. (Vibrators produce the most intense orgasms; oral and manual stimulation are rated second; and coital stimulation produces the least intense orgasms, according to statistics).
8. Multiple orgasms may be spaced by a few seconds or a few minutes.
9. Many women find that they feel completely satisfied with one orgasm.

female sexuality

10. There is no "right way" to have an orgasm. That means you don't *have* to have an orgasm during intercourse, and that orgasm achieved through oral or manual stimulation or with a vibrator is valid. Women have the right to decide how they prefer to have thier orgasms.

11. A woman can initiate sex. She'll enjoy it more if she feels confident she can give her partner pleasure, that she has some skills, and knows what her partner likes.

12. The sex act doesn't have to end after a male partner has ejaculated. If a woman still wants to continue she can stimulate herself or invite her partner to participate in any way that feels good.

13. A woman must feel that she can take time during sex for her own pleasure.

14. Having sex during a menstrual period is perfectly normal and okay. Many women feel more turned on around the time of their period. There is more pelvic congestion during this time. Having sex and/or orgasms can make a woman feel particularly good at this time. Orgasms may also relieve cramping.

15. *Lubrication* during sexual excitement varies greatly among women depending on many factors (state of health, birth control method, mood, partner, setting, turn-on level, etc.). There is no standard "right amount" of lubrication. Many women lubricate during the excitement phase and find lubrication diminishing if intercourse goes on for very long. Your own saliva or a bland lubricant, applied to the genitals, can greatly reduce friction and increase sexual pleasure. (See the list of lubricants, p. 124.)

16. Women don't need to be married to enjoy sex.

17. Making sounds can greatly enhance one's sexual experience.

18. Friction along the ceiling of the vagina can be enjoyable.

19. A feeling of fullness (deep penetration) can add to sexual pleasure.

20. Some women have cervixes which are sensitive, and like to be stimulated there by penis, finger, or dildo.

About faking orgasms

We've done it in the past because: marriage manuals told us to in order to keep our men and to seem like mature women. We didn't want our partners to know we didn't reach orgasm, for the sake of protecting his/her and our own ego. We were not sure what an orgasm was.

The effect of faking is that: orgasm remains a mystery if we aren't willing to look at it honestly; if we can't be honest we can't discuss our needs with our partners, so the situation doesn't improve. Our partners are confused about what a real response is. Our partners may not have any idea that things could be changed and improved.

The facts are that: the energy expended and wasted in faking could be channeled into experiencing the moment-by-moment pleasure we are receiving. Focusing on what's going on instead of on what *should be* going on is more likely to bring about orgasm. Once we share our wishes with our partner then both people can learn together how to improve the situation. Women are capable of having orgasms in about four minutes (according to Kinsey). Arousal rate depends on the effectiveness of stimulation and the desire to prolong the pleasurable sensations. Women no longer have to hope the man will do it for them.

OPTIONS

1. Women can have orgasms any way they prefer.

2. A woman can decide if she wants her orgasm(s) before intercourse, during intercourse, and/or afterwards.

3. A woman can define her own sexual lifestyle. Many women today find that there is a wide variety of lifestyles, one or more of which fit their individual needs. Some women are choosing long-term marriage contracts; some are choosing "open marriages" which include outside relationships. Some relationships last a short time and some last a long time. Some women are choosing to live together with their partners; some prefer to live alone or

in groups. Some relationships are monogamous. Some women don't want a primary partner at all. Some women are choosing to relate to partners of the same sex, and some women prefer to have sex with themselves exclusively. There are times when women don't want sex at all.

4. A woman can experience pleasure in sex without necessarily having an orgasm.

TECHNIQUES

The surest way to discover what turns you on and produces an orgasm is to masturbate.

1. Some women masturbate the same way every time.

2. Some women have a variety of techniques to choose from.

3. Most women use some combination of strokes on the clitoris and/or inner lips, in a variety of rhythms, with a variety of pressures, and different fingers or parts of the hands.

4. Some women stroke up and down, some sideways, back and forth, some in circles. Most concentrate on the moist, sensitive parts of their genitals.

5. Some women use a lubricant.

6. Some women stroke other parts of the body besides the genitals: breasts, chest, thighs, arms, face, or hips.

7. Some women press their thighs together in such a way as to create a pressure on their genitals; some women stimulate the clitoris by pressing the legs together.

8. Some women lie on a pillow or rub their genitals on the bed.

9. Some women have orgasms in the bath tub or shower by running water over the vulva.

10. Some women use vibrators

11. Some women use dildos.

(See also: *Masturbation*; and *Enrichment Techniques with Partners*.)

Some Helpful Books on Female Sexuality

Barbach, Lonnie. *For Yourself: The Fulfillment of Female Sexuality.* New York: Doubleday, 1975. Cloth, $7.95. "A guide to orgasmic response." Educates woman to her own body. Lists reasons for past sources of confusion, the role of partners, helpful exercises to do at home. Ms. Barbach shares insights from pre-orgasmic women's groups held in a university research setting.

Bengis, Ingrid. *Combat in the Erogenous Zone.* New York: Bantam, 1972. Paper, $1.95. One woman's account of the many episodes in her life that have made her hate both men and women, as well as her joys with both. She wrote this book to show how women often (if not always) have mixed feelings about men and each other, and how often the feelings transcend gender. The book is autobiographical, and doesn't come to any conclusions, but offers much to think about and discuss.

Boston Women's Health Collective. *Our Bodies, Ourselves: A Book by and for Women.* New York: Simon & Schuster, 1973. Paper, $2.95. This is a classic women's health book, covering the anatomy and physiology of reproduction, sexuality, being gay, living with others, nutrition, self-defense, rape, V.D., birth control, abortion, having children, menopause, and health care. It is a very useful household reference book and a strong feminist statement.

Hite, Shere. *Sexual Honesty: By Women For Women.* New York: Warner Paperback Library, 1974. Paper, $1.50. "Written anonymously by women 14-64 in response to a nationwide questionnaire on their sexuality." This

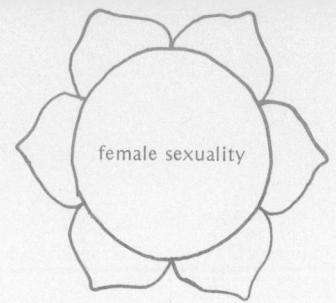

is the first book in a series intended to provide an open forum for women to honestly share the nature of their sexuality. Reflects the fact that women's sexuality may be a whole new concept just beginning to emerge in its own right as women end the ban on talking about sex. Includes the questionnaire used.

Millett, Kate. *Sexual Politics.* New York: Avon, 1971. Paper, $2.95. A classic analysis of the theory of sexual politics and the sexual revolution since 1830. There is a fine critical examination of Freud and his followers. The quotations and analysis are quite strong.

Rush, Anne Kent. *Getting Clear: Body Work for Women.* Westminster, N.Y.: Random House–Bookworks, 1973. Paper, $4.95. This book combines gestalt, yoga, the martial arts, rolfing, medical research, dance, other cultures. For both men and women interested in knowing themselves and their bodies better. There are sections on body work, exercises, relationships, therapy, massage, pelvic self-exams, and consciousness-raising. An excellent home reference book.

Sherfey, Mary Jane. *The Nature and Evolution of Female Sexuality.* New York: Random House, 1972. Paper, $1.95. This book traces the development of femaleness, pointing out that the fetus begins as female. She also expounds her theory that women's sexual drive has been forcibly suppressed to allow civilization to evolve.

c

LESBIANISM

A Lesbian is a woman whose primary interpersonal interests—emotionally, psychologically, socially, and sexually—are centered in another woman (or other women), whether or not these interests are ever expressed overtly.

This definition refutes one of the many myths still floating around about women homosexuals: that Lesbians are merely women who have sex with other women. Lesbians are not Lesbians simply because of the sexual aspects of their lives. Homosexual love, like heterosexual and bisexual love, is a complex, multifaceted phenomenon. Unfortunately over the years the so-called "experts" on the subject have put all the stress on the three letters in the middle of homo*sex*uality.

Actually, Lesbians are a cross-section of all women, from every racial, religious, educational, and socio-economic group. Roughly, they comprise 10 percent of the female population of the country, which means that there are in excess of ten million Lesbians in the United States. This is a sizable minority and a severely oppressed one, but because of the diverse nature of the Lesbian population and because many feel they must conceal their true natures in order to protect their families and jobs, organizing in a concerted drive for equal rights has been difficult. Still, Lesbians have been active in the women's movement from the start, since equal rights for women certainly are of concern to them. They are also working with their brothers in the gay liberation movement and with their sisters in the gay women's movement, in educating the society (and themselves) to the true nature of gay women. Slowly but surely, the myths and lies about gay women and men that have haunted our society for so long are breaking down.

One such myth is that homosexual women have it better in our society than homosexual men. This impression probably results from the fact that most investigation into homosexuality has been concerned with men—after all, ours is a male-centered culture. The fact is that Lesbians are doubly discriminated against: because they are homosexual and because they are women.

The following are some of the other myths about Lesbians that persist in our society:

Myth: Lesbianism is a second-best choice. Women become Lesbians when they can't get a man because they are so ugly.

Fact: For Lesbians, Lesbianism is the only choice. Many Lesbians have been heterosexually married or have at least tried out the other sex. To answer the other part of the myth all you need to do is look around a group of Lesbians. They are beautiful, pretty, homely, ugly. They are fat, stout, thin, or "just right." They are super-intelligent, intelligent, smart, not so smart, or dumb. Recently a number of researchers conducted comparative studies of the personalities of Lesbian and heterosexual women. None found any clear-cut differences between the two groups.

Myth: When two Lesbians get together, one plays the male ("butch") role and the other plays the female ("femme") role.

Fact: When two Lesbians get together that means two *women* are getting together. With a very few exceptions, Lesbian women live with partners on a non-role-playing basis, striving for as egalitarian a relationship as is possible between two human beings. A small minority of Lesbians do fall into the trap of imitating heterosexual couples.

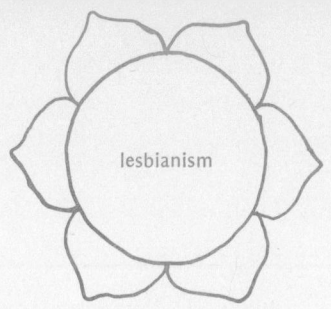

lesbianism

Myth: All Lesbians are man-hating dykes.

Fact: Lesbians do not hate men per se. They merely prefer women. However, *all* women, if they would admit it, are subject to a touch of man-hating. This is inevitable in a male-dominated society. And male attitudes toward women are evidence that woman-hating exists, too, in at least equal measure.

Myth: Lesbians must use dildos (penis substitutes) in lovemaking in order to be satisfied.

Fact: This is a male fantasy. Although no formal research has been done on this subject, informal surveys among Lesbians seldom find anyone who has used a dildo or who knows anyone who has used one. The ways two women can seek and find sexual gratification are limited only by their imagination. The three most common techniques, which can be performed by the partners simultaneously or in turn, are mutual masturbation (manipulation of the clitoris, caressing the labia and/or penetration of the vagina by the fingers); cunnilingus (stimulation of the same area by the tongue); tribadism (one woman lying atop the other, followed by up and down rhythmic motions to stimulate the clitoris of each). It should be pointed out that Alfred Kinsey and his colleagues and Masters and Johnson (among many) have noted that the surest way for a woman to achieve orgasm is through masturbation. Oral-genital stimulation is rated second, and penile thrusting is third.

Myth: Lesbians are promiscuous and never achieve lasting or worthwhile relationships.

Fact: Lesbians are women and therefore when they realize their sexual preference they bring with them all the conditioning they have received as women in our anti-sexual culture. Many, many Lesbians have formed long-lasting relationships based solely on love and commitment, since there are no legal ties to bind two women together as in heterosexual marriage. Other Lesbians have chosen to live alone or communally with a number of other women. As with heterosexuals, the scope of a Lesbian's sexual activity depends on her age, her background, her companions, and her world view.

Despite the progress made by the gay liberation movement in the past twenty years, there is still considerable anti-homosexual bias in this country. Dr. George Weinberg, in his book *Society and the Healthy Homosexual*, describes this harmful prejudice as *homophobia*, or an unreasoning fear of homosexuality. As a result of this fear of the unknown, Lesbians are fired from their jobs regardless of their work performance; parents disown their daughters, often because of their fear of what their friends and neighbors will say; "friends" are lost simply because they discover someone they have known, and liked, is a Lesbian; and Lesbian mothers lose custody of their children.

In the latter instance, some progress has been made and a few Lesbian mothers have been given custody of their children although they were open about their Lesbianism. However, most courts, usually presided over by white, male, heterosexual judges, deny custody to the mother solely because of her sexual preference. This is an extreme example of homophobia, based on the false concept that children raised by a homosexual will grow up gay (as if that were a fate worse than death). The courts fail to comprehend that at least 95 percent of all homosexuals are raised by heterosexual parents, and don't grow up heterosexual.

Most sex researchers agree that sexual identity is determined sometime between the ages of two and eight. Society, however, tends to assume that all children (whatever their ages) are non-sexual but will grow up to be heterosexual. This assumption places an extreme burden on the teenager who recognizes her Lesbian orientation. Teenagers particularly need to discuss their feelings with someone who will be understanding and non-judgmental. Usually the young woman knows that she has Lesbian feelings, but does not know how to meet others like herself, or how (or if) to tell her parents or friends. Loneliness, alienation, and confusion during the teenage years is extensive and little if anything has been done to work with this age group.

Despite society's homophobia, however, more and more Lesbians are "coming out." That is, they are announcing to parents, friends, co-workers, and sometimes to the public at large that they are Lesbian, happy, and proud. By being open they free themselves from the intolerable oppression of leading a double life, and they help dispel the myths of Lesbianism by confronting people with the facts.

For Lesbians, Lesbianism is a happy, productive, creative and viable lifestyle—just like heterosexuality can be for heterosexuals. Recognition of this fact will go a long way towards enabling our society to accept the diversity of people and the right of all persons to live and love in the way that is best for them.

The following books are suggested if you wish to become more acquainted with the lifestyle of the Lesbian:

Abbott, Sidney and Barbara Love. *Saphho was a Right-On Woman: A Liberated View of Lesbianism.* New York: Stein & Day, 1972. Paper, $1.95. An historical examination of Lesbianism plus a strongly militant view of how the liberation of gay women can be the keystone for the liberation of all people.

Martin, Del and Phyllis Lyon. *Lesbian/Woman.* San Francisco: Glide Publications, 1972. Cloth, $7.95. New York: Bantam, 1972. Paper, $1.50. A personal account by two women who have lived together for twenty-two years and have been active in the Lesbian movement for twenty years. This best-seller is written from personal experience as well as extensive research.

Martin, Del and Phyllis Lyon. *Lesbian Love and Liberation.* San Francisco: Multi Media Resource Center. Paper, $1.95. One of the volumes in the *YES Book of Sex* series. This is an introduction to Lesbian lifestyles. Photographs by women of the Lesbian community are included.

Klaich, Dolores. *Woman Plus Woman, Attitudes Toward Lesbianism.* New York: Simon & Schuster, 1974. Cloth, $8.95. Covers the history of the Lesbian as well as the lives of some well-known women who were Lesbians. Excellent interviews with contemporary Lesbians about their lives and lifestyles.

Rosen, David H., M.D. *Lesbianism: A Study of Female Homosexuality.* Springfield, Ill.: Charles C. Thomas, 1974. Cloth, $7.95. Paper, $3.95. Reviews the literature, presents twenty-six case studies, and concludes with a discussion on Lesbianism and psychiatric treatment. A positive view of Lesbianism as a "way of life" by a medical man.

BISEXUALITY: SELF-DEFINITION AND ANDROGYNY

SELF-DEFINITION

At this point we can begin to consider the options in lifestyle available to every human being seeking to enrich his or her own sexuality. We start by exploring bisexuality because it is all-embracing. For the hetero- or homosexual, bisexuality represents an expansion, rather than a shift, in consciousness.

Sexual lifestyles are a matter of choice. A hetero-, homo-, or bisexual person defines him- or herself as such. Many people define their sexuality by default; that is, they submit to society's pressure and make no choice at all. But with the crippling Victorian morality finally giving way to the individual's right to decide, these people are discovering that all forms of sexuality are available to everyone. They are starting to understand that the choice to explore other modes of sexual expression is open to them at any point in their lives. Bisexuality, then, is not an objective "condition"; it is a subjective experience. It is a self-defined place.

Loving ourselves is the most fundamental and basic sexual love affair we can have. By being truly turned on to ourselves we can feel free to respond to others. Second only to loving ourselves is sexually loving *anyone* we care for, regardless of their sex. It may be that if we were truly unafraid of our own and other people's bodies, and not intimidated by our prior conditioning, we would all be naturally bisexual. Were this the case, it is easy to imagine some people choosing to be homosexual and some choosing to be heterosexual on the basis of individual preference developed through experience rather than through conditioning.

Who is bisexual? Anyone who informs you that she or he is. Any other definition won't work. One theory holds that fantasies are the measure by which to judge. Thus, if a person is sexual with men but fantasizes about women and men, that person may be considered bisexual. But this theory does not allow for the crucial element of self-definition. In our terms, then, a bisexual is a person who consciously defines her- or himself *as* a bisexual.

Many people find peace and resolution to their sexual conflicts by expressing themselves bisexually. They often find that their sense of security cannot be induced by outside determinants: "I can't rely on anyone else to define my world; none of the homo- or hetero- role models fit; my sense of *home* is something I must generate for myself." The expanded range of possible sexual identities and actions that the bisexual embraces is often a welcome relief from stereotypic roles for people who have felt restricted or unsatisfied. Often, since anyone cared about is a potential partner, they no longer feel the need to compete for sexual attention or act out their sexual insecurities through possessiveness and jealousy.

Being bisexual may not be for everyone, but those who have grown or would like to grow into it, whether they come from a straight or gay orientation, believe that bisexuality is the fullest expression of human sexuality because it is not an either/or orientation, but a living out of both/and. It is a state in which people can live and grow, reaching out with warmth and openness to all individuals they care about, regardless of the structure of their genitals. It means feeling comfortable with both men and women, not only sexually, but also sensually, emotionally, and intellectually.

Some people feel that the bisexual is a perverse polygamist, and that bisexuality engenders possessiveness, jealousy, and envy. Bi people are sometimes urged to "come out," to make a choice. We feel that much of the prejudice against bisexuality results from people's *fear of each other* sexually, *fear of their bodies*, and that this fear creates great anger and more fear, violence, and so on. The fear of one's own body is one of the most crippling forms of self-hatred endured by human sexuals.

The women's and gay liberation movements have done much to encourage and enable a large number of people to "come out." But these movements have dichotomized the possibilities. They imply that the only choice is between gay *or* straight modes of sexual expression. But bisexuality is a very real option available to all human beings. Perhaps it is the most enriching and fulfilling—the most human—option of all.

There is no law that says a person must remain loyal to her or his first-tried mode of sexual expression. Bisexuality can represent a balance between the polarization of gay and straight ways of life. Sometimes this balance can be found in a primary relationship that is honest and open and accepts other partners for either or both persons in the primary. In this way, for example, a heterosexual primary relationship can be maintained while both partners enjoy other forms of sexual expression.

The needs for security and permanence are very real, but they are not necessarily met by monogamy and possessiveness. A person who is unwillingly involved in a monogamous relationship can feel that his or her true self is being dissolved. Bisexuals are attracted to *people*, not necessarily to penises or clitorises; their style of life implies that people can love and enjoy other people without owning and imprisoning them.

ANDROGYNY

Each of us has the right to decide who our friends and sex partners will be, not according to a set of principles, but on the basis of that indefinable "turn-on"—the feeling that this person is someone special. As we learn to conduct ourselves according to our own choices and not according to our power to dominate, sex roles—what we have learned to call masculinity and femininity—become less important. We find that it is possible, and more comfortable, to be androgynous.

Androgyny usually means having the qualities of both male and female. In a feminist sense, it means having the non-sexist qualities of a human being, the core that remains when the sexual characteristics decreed by society are pared away. With less concentration on developing the "masculine" and "feminine" parts of our personalities, we become ever more androgynous. The point is not to separate our masculine and feminine characteristics, but to allow them to merge naturally into an unlimited *human* personality. Out of this new freedom the tendency toward bisexuality grows.

At this point in time it may be easier for women to be bisexual than it is for men, since women have always been allowed by society to form close relationships without necessarily dominating each other. But the women's movement is educating men as well as women to the fact that satisfying human relationships are based upon mutual choice and not upon dominance and submission.

"If it were not for the social brainwashing and cultural taboos, most people could relate sexually to people of both sexes . . ."

> Lonnie Myers, M.D.
> Sex Educator, Chicago

"Bisexual men (and women) are here; they refuse to stay in any one corner. In taking away the societal fears, they could help all persons be able to reach out comfortably to each other."

> Don Clark, Ph.D.
> Lecturer, Author

"It is a characteristic of the human mind to dichotomize human sexual behavior. Also many persons don't want to believe that there might be gradations of sexual choice, and that there *are*, in fact, bisexuals."

> Alfred Kinsey, et al.
> *Sexual Behavior in the Human Male*

bisexuality

"If the state controls sexuality, it controls everything."

Wilhelm Reich, M.D.

"The human mind invents such categories as hetero- and homo- and tries to force facts into separated pigeonholes. The living world is a continuum in all of its aspects. The sooner we learn that this applies to human sexual behavior, the sooner we shall reach a sound understanding of the realities of sex."

Alfred Kinsey, et al.
Sexual Behavior in the Human Male

"Bisexual women may make the most important contribution to not only the women's movement, but also to the whole field of human sexuality."

Sidney Abbott and Barbara Love
Sappho Was a Right-On Woman

CHILDREN

The Kinsey data revealed that almost all kids go through a gay period when they are young, but that this form of expression gets crushed as the adult world makes increasing demands for adolescent conformity and intellectual decision-making. If both gay and straight feelings were allowed to develop naturally, perhaps there would be many more self-identified bisexuals today.

Children's same-sex feelings are natural.

The best thing bisexuals can do in regard to their children is to be very clear and comfortable with their own sexuality. This will, more than anything, free their children to make their own feelings and actions consonant with each other.

Whether parents choose bi, gay, or hetero modes of relating, children should be allowed to develop the self-defining and self-determining aspects of their personalities unfettered by familial or societal pressures. Children should be allowed to grow to maturity feeling good about themselves, their bodies, and their own chosen sexual identifications.

LET'S GET BEYOND LABELS

We are learning to fit spontaneously into situations with people without worrying about what our "label" "should" be. The new androgyny means more than coming out of the closet and into the street; it also means coming out of our antiquated attic fantasies and into the world of real people and their sexuality.

Wherever we may end up, for the time being we can view bisexuality as an oasis, a resting place from restrictive definitions. Or perhaps we should see it as a path towards more open, freely expressed human sexuality based on personal preference resulting from experience. Bisexuals are not copping out; they are copping in. They want to have their cake and eat it too, and why not? They have chosen to keep all options open, to explore all possibilities. The bisexual attitude toward sex is an attitude toward life: having freed themselves from restrictive definitions, bisexuals want to live as much as possible in freedom and fulfillment.

Bisexuals are not paragons. They are not necessarily free of conflict, sexually or otherwise, but they are struggling to integrate their lives. We hope that the liberation movement will free all of us from the need to cling to labels. Labels are an easy target for repressive forces. Let's call ourselves human beings.

"the time has come, I think, when we must recognize Bisexuality as a normal form of human behavior."

Margaret Mead, Ph.D.
Redbook Magazine
January, 1975

CELIBACY: ANOTHER OPTION

Most of us have been taught that we need an intense relationship with a person of the opposite gender in order to be whole people. To a great extent we are taught to define ourselves in terms of others. Sometimes we may get lost in the shuffle. A self-determined period of celibacy may give us the space to develop a more meaningful relationship with ourselves. It can give us the privacy, integrity, time and energy to devote to determining our needs and wants. This often results in better relationships with others.

Some people define celibacy to include masturbation. Others would exclude masturbation. Either way, masturbation can be a way into and out of a celibate period.

Touching and intimacy can still be a part of our interaction with others even when or if we choose not to have sex.

VIDEO—WEEK 2.

"A GAY VIEW/MALE" tells the problems of growing up in a sex role stereotype. The film makes the points that coming to terms with homosexual feelings is a task for all men and that being gay is much more than just a sexual experience.

"VIR AMAT." Note the playful element of this sexual encounter. Tenderness and loving looks are the sexual signals.

"TITLES AVAILABLE." Sing along with Bill. Saying the words takes the sting out.

"RICH AND JUDY." The buildup of excitation (turn-on) stage and all four phases of the sexual response cycle are visible in this film. Note the partners' playfulness.

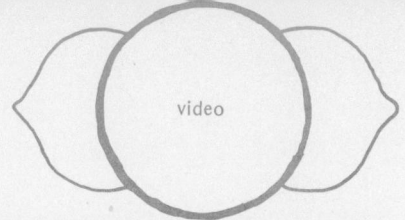

"FREE." About choosing a place, eating "turn-on" foods before sex, and joyfulness and celebration.

"SUN BRUSHED." Note the aliveness and freedom of the woman in "top" position, and the integration of the orgasm with environmental sounds. Pay particular attention to mutual oral-genital pleasuring, and see how stroking and massage is integrated with sex action.

"FULLNESS" explores intercourse during pregnancy—anal intercourse, oral stimulation, caresses, and tenderness and appreciation of bodies through touching and stroking.

"JOY IN HER PLEASURE" focuses on the participant pleasurer, a woman who guides the man towards her pleasure. Note the orgasmic intensity of the woman and their mutual joy in her orgasm.

C

"CLOSING THE CIRCLE." Two men and a woman bridge the sexual gap, the men relating to each other. They also reach across the generation gap; the younger man *could be* the son of the other two. Great caring and affection is shown by all three people. The woman takes the lead.

AT HOME EXERCISE

	Section C Page No.

With Yourself:

14.	Masturbate in a New Way	97
15.	Light Stroking	98
16.	Incorporating Pelvic Breathing with Masturbation	98
17.	Yeses and Nos	99
18.	Productive/Non-productive Hour	100
19.	Sex Words	101

With Partner:

20.	Three Things to Change	102
21.	Intercourse in a New Position	102
22.	Intercourse with Additional Stimulation	102

Repeat Exercises:

Breathing Exercises 2a, 2i.
Sensory Awareness Exercises 3a, 3b

Don't neglect your journal.

Read Ahead for Next Week:

Massage, p. 106.
Reread Female Sexuality, Lesbianism, Bisexuality, if desired.

AT HOME EXERCISE 14—MASTURBATE IN A NEW WAY

A lot of people masturbate pretty much the same way every time. The more we learn to vary the stimuli, the more possibilities are open to us to increase our pleasure, and the less chance there is of getting "in a rut." During this exercise try to find at least *one new* way to masturbate enjoyably. Experiment with as many of the following suggestions as you can during your daily hour. Remember the *goal* is to create a new sensation for yourself, not to have an orgasm. If you have an orgasm, fine, but it's okay if the new experience doesn't cause an orgasm.

1. Try a different place; a different room, outside in a private place, a rocking chair, the shower, the floor, etc.
2. Make at least one change in the atmosphere of your space: lights lower, lights higher, colored lights, different music, different scents, a mirror, a picture.
3. Experiment with changing the time of day during which you masturbate. Try doing it when you wake up, during the day, after lunch, before a date, before an important meeting or a test.
4. Change from the hand you usually use. Use both hands.
5. Change your body position. Try sitting, standing, kneeling, legs apart, legs together, on your stomach, on your back, on your side, with your buttocks propped up on a pillow, sitting in lotus position.
6. Change to a different fantasy, if you have fantasies.
7. Experiment with other things besides your hands and fingers: vibrator, running water, a piece of fur, a silk scarf, leather, a feather, textured objects.
8. Try a different kind of lubrication, oil, creme, saliva, etc., see the list of lubricants in the appendix, p. 124.

AT HOME EXERCISE 15—LIGHT STROKING

The light stroking exercise is designed to help expand your perception of different kinds of touches. It is aimed at sensitizing your whole genital area, not at producing an orgasm.

Spend the first twenty minutes of your hour very lightly stroking all around your genitals with a touch like a feather. In fact, you might try using a feather. Vary the direction and length of the strokes, trying to get a sense of just barely touching yourself. Again, don't neglect your anus. Be aware that you don't have to go anywhere with this stroking; just focus on the sensations. After twenty minutes, finish your masturbation hour in the way that feels best to you.

AT HOME EXERCISE 16—INCORPORATE PELVIC BREATHING INTO MASTURBATION

Work on coordinating breathing and masturbation. As you inhale, lying on your back or standing up, press your behind down or back; as you exhale, thrust upwards or forward with your pelvis. Practice very carefully so that you begin to do it this way automatically rather than vice versa!

As you become more and more aroused through masturbation it is vitally important to continue your rhythmic breathing and relax into the mounting tensions. This will gradually enable you to bring more and more of your total body into your sexual response pattern.

AT HOME EXERCISE 17—YES & NO

Often in the course of our daily lives we forget to meet our own needs because we are busy making sure everyone else or everything else is taken care of. Often, when it comes to what we want, we are hesitant to say a definite YES or a definite NO to things we want to do or are asked to do. Try this exercise and see if it helps to change this, if it makes it easier for you to get what you want out of life.

NO's

Say "no" to at least three things that you would normally do grudgingly. This may be something you feel you "should" do but really don't want to. It is important that you say "no" to somebody other than yourself for one of your NO's.

Select things you would not normally allow yourself to refuse, for example, a social "obligation," letting the dog in, jiggling the toilet, etc.

YES's

Say "yes" to three things you really want but would not ordinarily allow yourself to have or allow yourself to ask others for. For example, a raise, a room of your own, a ride somewhere, a gift for yourself, a vacation, a new position.

Try to start with little things and *do three YES's and three NO's a week*. Do them at work, at home, at school, wherever you are. As you get more comfortable with non-sexual requests and refusals, begin to incorporate one NO and one YES that is sexual each week.

You are cheating if (1) you say "no" to something you want but still think you "shouldn't" have; (2) you say "no" or "yes" to things you ordinarily or always say "no" or "yes" to.

Experience the feeling after saying your YES's and NO's. Try not to worry about the other person's needs and don't let them influence what *you* want. The goal of the exercise is to be more self-assertive.

Many opportunities will present themselves for this YES or NO exercise. If you let an opportunity go by and don't say anything, don't become discouraged. Make a mental note of how often you deny yourself to others or don't allow yourself to do things you want to do. If it's harder for you to say YES, practice the YES exercise. If it's harder for you to say NO practice the NO's.

YES's for this week

NO's for this week

AT HOME EXERCISE 18 — PRODUCTIVE/NON-PRODUCTIVE HOUR

Take a minute or two to rate yourself on a scale of 1 to 10 as follows:

One (1) means that you are always busy, compulsively doing things that are "productive": homework, housework, hobbies, civic affairs, children, mending, fixing up, odd jobs, etc.

Ten (10) means that you rarely, if ever, do anything "productive." You mostly sit around, or lie around, doing nothing or watching TV.

Five (5) would be right in the middle, a perfect balance.

Got your number now? OK.

If your number is between 1 and 5, your assignment is to think of something that you want to do that is totally non-productive. You can sit and do absolutely nothing if you like. Get in touch with how it feels to have nothing to do during this time. Let your mind just float; as ideas and thoughts come into it let them pass right on out. This is not a time to plan your grocery list or figure your capital gains tax or mend leotards. Recall the last time you spent an hour doing nothing, being non-productive.

If your number is between 5 and 10, decide on something that you would enjoy doing that will accomplish something. Finish a project that has been on your mind. Do whatever interests you, but be sure you choose something that you can finish. Then be aware of how you feel about yourself when you have done it. Think about the last time you set out to do something and finished it and remember how you felt then.

AT HOME EXERCISE 19—SEX WORDS

Write your own sex words for

ORAL SEX

INTERCOURSE

PETTING

OTHER

MASTURBATION

C

101

AT HOME EXERCISE 20—THREE THINGS TO CHANGE (PARTNER)

This is an exercise in communication designed to facilitate more direct communication about the changes you and your partner want to make. First decide with your partner on a time and place to do this exercise.

A. Write down in your journal three things you would like to change in order to improve things sexually *for yourself*. Then write down three things you think your partner could change to improve sex *for you*.

B. After you and your partner have written your lists down in your journals individually, read your lists aloud to each other. Discuss the new things you have learned about yourself and your partner. Each of you should decide on one thing you are going to change. The TALKING AND LISTENING exercise format (page 68) will be helpful in doing this section of the exercise.

AT HOME EXERCISE 21—INTERCOURSE IN A NEW POSITION (PARTNER)

Positions used during intercourse can make a difference in the type of sensation a person receives and gives. Some positions create intensified sensations for one partner and some positions create more intense sensations for the other. Many couples use more than one position in the process of intercourse. Words cannot describe as well as pictures can the endless possibilities of two people making love with one another. Experiment with at least one new way to have intercourse.

AT HOME EXERCISE 22—INTERCOURSE WITH ADDITIONAL STIMULATION (PARTNER)

Our bodies have many sensitive areas which may not receive adequate stimulation during intercourse in the positions we usually use. Adequate and effective stimulation is needed to reach orgasm. The purpose of this exercise is to find one new position for intercourse that allows both ourselves and our partner to touch some of these areas.

Men often particularly enjoy strokes on the shaft of the penis and the testicles or anus. Women often like touch on the clitoris, inner lips or anus. Since most women find the clitoris is the most sexually sensitive part of the body, it is especially important that it receive stimulation during intercourse.

Determine which parts of your body would like more touch and find a position in the illustrations (or make one up) that leaves those parts free for touching. Take turns choosing positions to try until you have found one you especially like.

Spend 20 minutes experimenting with these new positions. You may then stop or go on to any other activity you want.

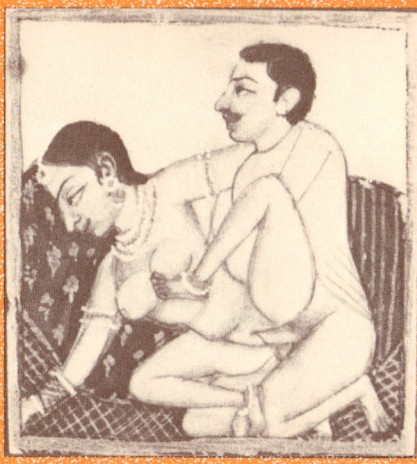
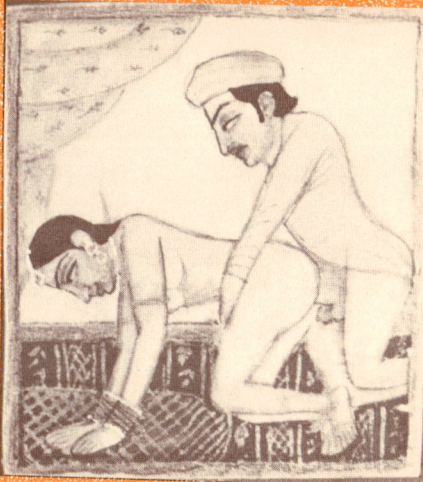
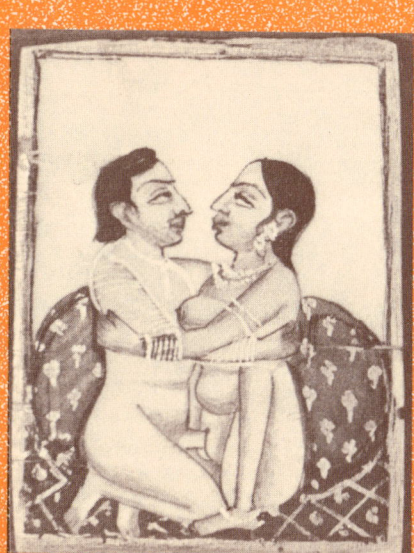
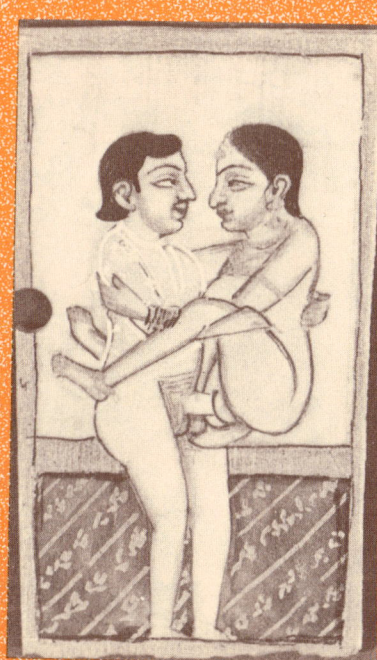

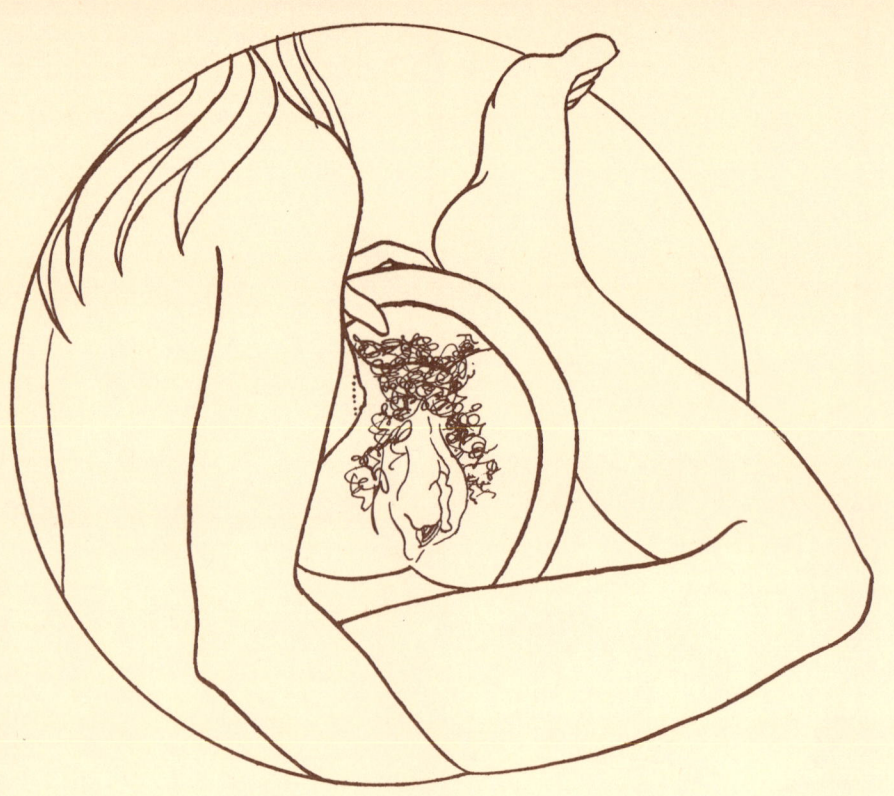

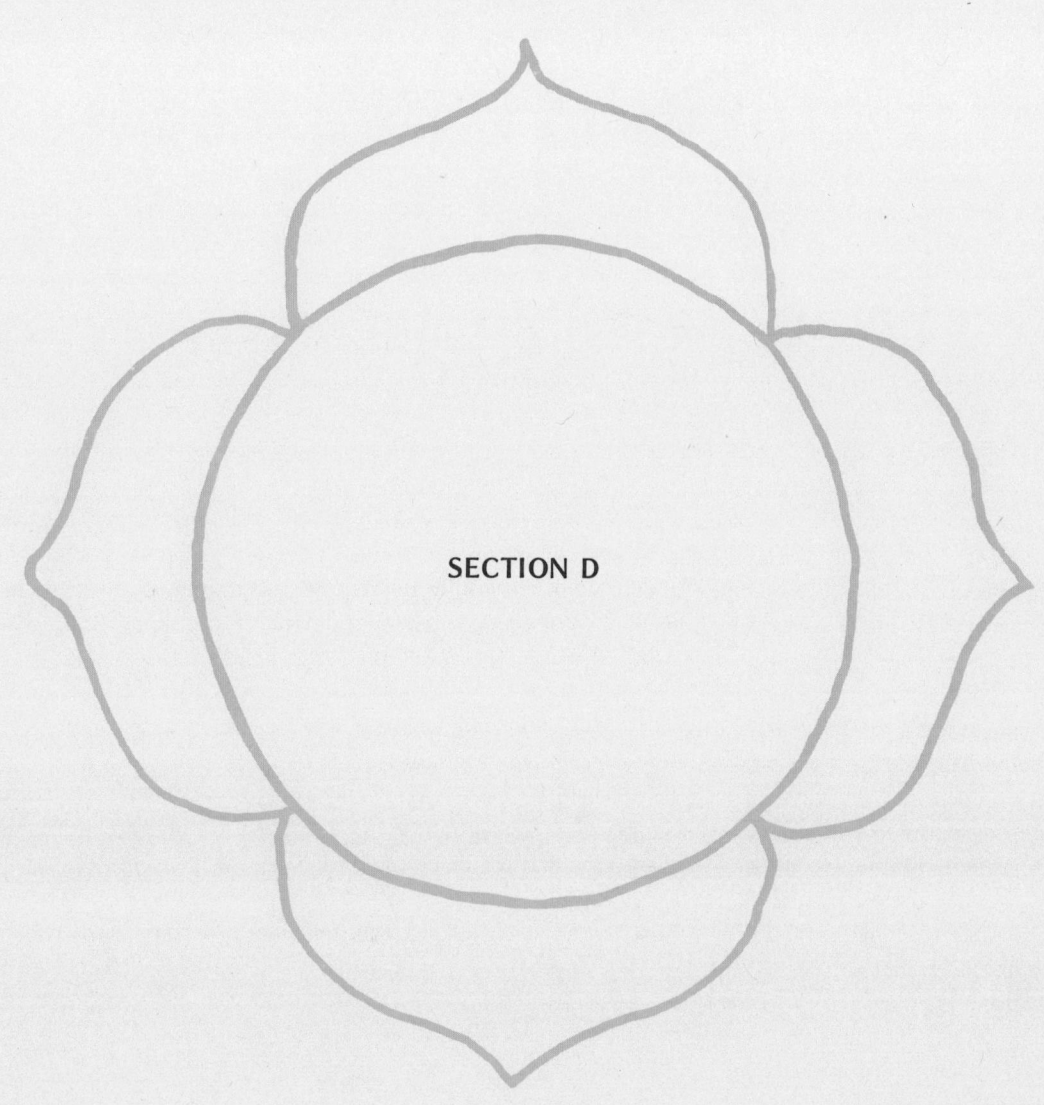

SECTION D

MASSAGE

Most of us have received very little instruction in the personal nurturing art of giving and receiving pleasure through touch. Because of this we can spend most of our lives starving for physical touching and closeness.

A little learning about touching often results in a large increase in the overall level of sexual pleasure. One very effective means of improving touching skills is through massage. What we mean by massage is caring and tender forms of touching and rubbing. There are many other forms of massage which focus on remedial treatment for persons with ailments. These latter are carried out by trained specialists.

The massage of caring and communicating feeling is a safe and pleasant way to create a comfortable space for receiving and giving pleasurable touches. The non-demand situation in massage can assist us in learning to speak to each other more openly and directly about our feelings, our experiences, and our appreciation of the other person.

Begin by looking into one of the massage books available. When you have found some things that you would like to try, put the books away and begin with your partner. Or begin by practicing on yourself, perhaps in the shower or bath. Spend some time practicing two or three strokes until you feel that they are as good as they can be. Give and receive lots of feedback when you are working with your partner. Then try adding new strokes to your massage, a few at a time, until you have learned as many as you like.

You can also take a short course in massage: a nice gift to yourself or to your partner. The best way to learn to give a good massage is to get one (another gift to yourself).

Massage may or may not be a sexual kind of experience. If you and your partner get turned on, fine. If not, that's okay too. If you do become aroused, savor the feelings and put off seeking sexual satisfaction during the first few sessions. This will enable you to appreciate more fully the feelings and responses and allow the massage experience to exist in its own right rather than being immediately incorporated into your sex life. After several sensual massage sessions, you may decide that massage fits in well with your sexual space, or you may not. Keep checking your partner's or friend's feelings on this.

In giving feedback, tell what you like and don't like; state what changes in touch (lighter, more pressure, slower) you would like; and tell your partner what would be more pleasurable.

The non-demand conditions of massage can help us learn to communicate at other times when our motivation is more urgent. When you give or receive a massage, concentrate your total attention to the experience of the hands on the body, the specific muscles and parts that are being touched. This will help you to attend to your sensations during sexual arousal (when senses become covered by other feelings). Many of us find new experiences of pleasurable touching too much to get used to all at once. Give yourself time to become accustomed to the new sensations and feelings.

Practice and enjoy.

Massage Bibliography

Downing, George. *The Massage Book* Illustrated by Anne Kent Rush. Westminster, Md.: Random House, 1972. Paper, $3.95. This well-known book on massage shows Esalen-style massage techniques. Sections include how to: make a table, massage yourself, massage your animals, massage your lover (explicit) and go further into meditation and other types of massage. Excellent detailed instructions.

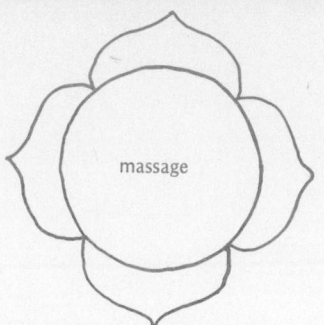

Gunther, Bernard. *Sense Relaxation Below Your Mind: A Book of Experiments in Being Alive.* New York: Pocket Books, 1973. Paper, $1.50. A book of exercises and games to do by yourself, with a partner, or in a group. The book tells what to do, makes suggestions and leaves the experiencing to you. A very fine handbook for people interested in relaxation and/or self-exploration.

Inkeles, Gordon and Murray Todris. *The Art of Sensual Massage.* Photos by Robert Foolthorap. San Francisco: Straight Arrow, 1972. Paper, $4.95. This is a how-to-do-it massage book that has lots of photographs of people giving and receiving massage.

Montague, Ashley. *Touching: The Human Significance of Skin.* New York: Harper and Row, 1971. Paper, $1.50. Montague points out the need for physical contact and stresses the importance of touching and stroking to physical growth and development, and the degree of physical intimacy as an adult.

Young, Constance. *Self Massage.* New York: Bantam, 1973. Paper, $.60. This is a tiny book on massage describing several styles. Massage is suggested for better health, for relaxation, and to heal headaches.

D

VIDEO—WEEK 3.

"IN WINTER LIGHT" examines the sexual pattern of two Lesbians. Each woman focuses on the sexual pleasure of the other. They experience their orgasms serially (one after the other). Stimulation is continued through the first orgasm and into the second. Note the differences between the two bodies, especially the musculature of the one and the facial transformation of the other during her orgasm. Pay attention to changes in breathing.

"A GAY VIEW/FEMALE." Three Lesbians discuss the realities of Lesbianism.

"BOTH/AND" is about sex-role self-definition. The sexual options are expanded to include relating emotionally, sensuously, and sexually to *both* women *and* men. These bisexual friends are comfortable with a group sexual setting.

"SEXOLOGICAL EXAM." This guided sexological examination in a home setting provides a format for communication of pleasure. Note the deepening of intimacy as the exam progresses. The film illustrates the steps for doing your home sexological.

"A RIPPLE IN TIME." The man is sixty-five; the woman fifty-two. They are taking their time. The woman pleasures herself during intercourse with a vibrator and with her hand. They use a variety of positions, each on top and sideways entry. Note especially the stuffing of the partially-erect penis into the vagina, the man's self-stimulation, their verbal communication, the woman's multiple orgasms, the timing of orgasm with an airplane sound, and the acting out of fantasy. Sex just keeps getting better as we get older; the woman's initiatory capacity matches the man's.

AT HOME EXERCISES

	Section D Page No.

With Yourself:

23.	Masturbation with Something in Your Vagina/ around Your Penis	110
24.	Sexual Experience Awareness and Rating Scale	110
25.	Secret Intent	111
26.	Get Something Sexy	111

With Partner:

27.	Home Sexological Exam	112
28.	Informational Massage	113
29.	Sharing Masturbation	114

Repeat Exercises

Pelvic Breathing with Masturbation Exercise 16
Yes's and No's Exercise 17

Breathing Exercises 2a, 2i
Sensory Awareness Exercises 3a, 3b
Kegel Exercise 4

Your Journal

Reread any sections you are not clear about.
Read the rest of the SARguide.

AT HOME EXERCISE 23—MASTURBATION WITH SOMETHING IN YOUR VAGINA/AROUND YOUR PENIS

Some women feel that they might like to feel something inside their vagina when they are masturbating, to create pressure. Some men feel that they would like to have something around their penis. You can experiment with different things and decide what feels best to you and just how and when you want to use them (at the beginning of masturbating, later on, just before orgasm, whenever you like).

Some women already have dildo-shaped vibrators; some like to go to the grocery store and check out the vegetable counter. Others prefer their own fingers inserted near the opening of the vagina. Decide for yourself and be creative.

Men sometimes like something furry, or soft and pliable (like a hot water bottle, soft leather or a towel) around their penis when they masturbate.

Whatever you use, be sure it is safe, especially if you place it inside your vagina or anus. Don't use glass, wood, or other hard materials.

Try using a bland lubricant (KY Jelly) during insertion. (See List of Lubricants in Appendix.)

Whatever you choose should be clean. Washing in soap and water is fine; rinse well. You can soak plastic objects in rubbing alcohol for about 20 minutes, then rinse well.

AT HOME EXERCISE 24—SEXUAL EXPERIENCE AWARENESS

Based on both psychologic reactions and overt experience, individuals rate as follows:

0. Exclusively heterosexual with no homosexual.
1. Predominantly heterosexual, only incidentally homosexual.
2. Predominantly heterosexual, but more than incidentally homosexual.
3. Equally heterosexual and homosexual.
4. Predominantly homosexual, but more than incidentally heterosexual.
5. Predominantly homosexual, only incidentally heterosexual.
6. Exclusively homosexual.

KINSEY'S HETEROSEXUAL-HOMOSEXUAL RATING SCALE

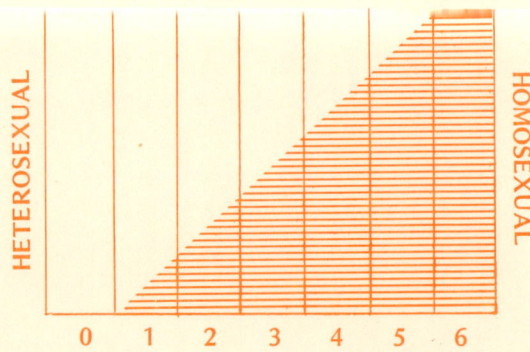

From *Sexual Behavior in the Human Male.*

Rate yourself.

Place an X on this scale where you fit in fantasy.

Place an O on this scale where you fit in activity.

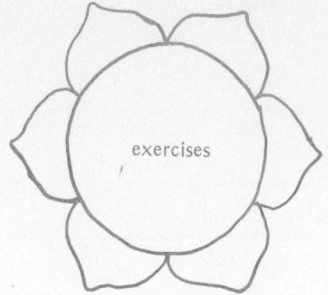

AT HOME EXERCISE 25—SECRET INTENT

This exercise is to be initiated after you have gained some experience in knowing your desires and setting realistic goals for yourself.

Concentrate on something erotic that you really want to do for yourself and that you can reasonably expect to accomplish during this week. The goal you are setting needs to be simple and specific. For example: I want to masturbate lying on my stomach; I want to masturbate while watching the "Tonight Show." Think about your goal and work with it until you can picture yourself doing it and have a clear picture of it in your mind. Then make a clear statement: "I will . . . "

Don't share your goal with anyone. Keep it to yourself.

Each morning when you wake up, repeat your goal to yourself. Repeat it again to yourself just before you go to sleep. Choose one five-minute time period each day to focus on your goal. During this five minutes (only five), sit in a comfortable position, take a few deep breaths, close your eyes and visualize first your goal and then all the steps leading up to it.

Determine how you will feel, what colors will be around you, what the scents will be, whether it will be warm or cold, how it will taste. Develop your image as much as you can in the five-minute period. After you have clearly pictured the goal in your mind, forget it. Each morning and night when you have clearly repeated your goal to yourself, forget it.

As your goal becomes clearer in your picture, you will find yourself doing things to bring it into existence. After a week or two, when you have accomplished your goal, report on it to your class or to your partner.

If you have selected a goal and find yourself not carrying it out, it is probably not your goal. It may be someone else's goal. Discard that goal and begin working on another in the same way.

D

AT HOME EXERCISE 26—GET SOMETHING SEXY

Quite often we like to express our sexual feelings in some sort of symbolic way. One way to do this is by adding something to your place—the private space you use for sexual activities—something that gets you in the mood or adds a sensual dimension to your mood or feeling. Try a candle, some incense, colored lights, African drum music (Olatunji), "mood music," a mirror placed just right, a picture or poster, massage oil, a heat lamp or heater, flowers, or some clothing to put on or take off. Discuss with your partner what things you can bring into your place that will enhance it for both of you. You and your partner might decide to each get something. Or perhaps you can decide on one "perfect thing" between you.

The action of doing this will be a step towards your own enhancement of your pleasure.

Make the place your intimate space expressing your own ideas of what is sexy and sensual.

AT HOME EXERCISE 27—HOME SEXOLOGICAL EXAMINATION

This exercise is designed to facilitate communication with our partners about our likes and dislikes for genital stimulation.

How to proceed:
1. Watch the Sexological Exam video tape.
2. Use genital diagrams following to mark sensitivity.
3. Take turns examining (person A) and being examined (person B).
4. Give each other plenty of specific feedback, be honest. Use some agreed upon system for designating pleasure, neutrality and unpleasure. You might use numbers or colors.
5. Spend some time at the beginning of each exam allowing person B to guide the hand of person A. Person A allows person B to be in charge for a few minutes. Person B takes person A's hand and places her or his hand on top of it, finger by finger. B then guides A's hand in the areas, strokes, rhythms, pressures he or she prefers.
6. Person A then spends some time giving the strokes she or he enjoys giving. Person B gives feedback.
7. Both may suggest new strokes.
8. Limit each exam period to 30 minutes. You may do both exams in this time or do one now and another a day or so later.
9. If you feel like having sex when you have finished your exam, wait at least 4 hours so that you can better allow yourself to focus on the education aspects.
10. Finish each exam with 10 minutes of spoon breathing (p. 39).

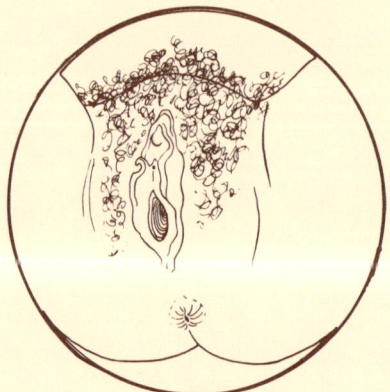 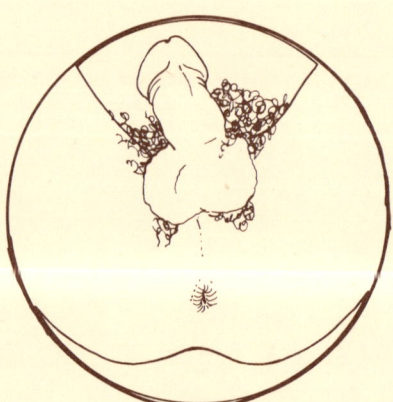

AT HOME EXERCISE 28—INFORMATIONAL MASSAGE

We often associate touching each other as a demand for, or a move toward, having sex. This expectation can sometimes create a situation where the only time we get touched is just before sex, and sometimes we miss out on touching just for the *pleasure* of being touched and caressed. Re-establishing feelings of closeness, affection and trust can be done through massage that does not lead to sex.

Set aside some time to explore how and where you like to touch and be touched.

With permission from a friend or partner, spend fifteen minutes stroking her or his body solely for your own pleasure. Ask the receiver to give feedback only if you cause discomfort or pain. Respect these limits.

Take a short break and then spend fifteen minutes touching your partner or friend for his or her pleasure. Ask for lots of feedback.

Is it easier for you to touch for your pleasure or the pleasure of another?

On another day, switch roles. Is it easier for you to give or receive?

D

AT HOME EXERCISE 29—SHARING MASTURBATION

Masturbating in the presence of a willing partner(s) provides us with another enrichment opportunity.

Each of us knows best what turns us on. Each person is best at providing the right kind of stimulation for her/his masturbation pleasure. Sharing information about your desires for specific kinds of stimulation is one of the most direct ways of teaching your partner(s) what you like and to learn what he/she likes.

Providing your own stimulation with a partner present can help you learn to take the responsibility for your own sexual patterns and needs. This can be a very helpful option when your partner is ill, tired, or just not sexually motivated. You can have your sexual turn-on and your partner's closeness without placing the burden of demand on the other. This is especially important in long-time ongoing relationships.

Also when your partner can provide some or all of his/her own sexual stimulation, you may begin to find it easier to focus on the pleasure of the sexual experience rather than on your performance.

Many people believe that their partner will be turned off by watching them masturbate, and fear that they will be rejected. This discomfort comes from all those negative societal messages that leave us feeling that masturbation is a "second-best" kind of sexual expression. We now know that this is not a fact, and that masturbation is potentially as good and rewarding an experience sexually as any other act. In actual fact, most people are turned on by watching their lovers masturbate, or watching someone they care for receiving sexual pleasure.

Begin by using the talking and listening exercise (p. 68), discussing this exercise on social masturbation. Then review the masturbation history from your journal (p. 69). Find a quiet time in your comfortable space and begin.

Some people like to start out with the other person in the house but not in the same room, as long as they both know what's happening. Others like the partner to hold them but to remain out of sight, perhaps with the lights very low. Others like plenty of light with the partner watching right from the start. Discuss this. Find the best way for you. Decide who will go first, and start.

As you feel more comfortable (however long that may take), you'll find it easier to focus on your feelings and sensations. Go at your own pace. If you're wondering what your partner's reactions are, what her/his feelings are, ask and check it out.

Practice will allow you to focus more and more on *your* turn-on, *your* stroking, and *your* pleasurable feelings and orgasms. Some people will find that they can't reach orgasm in this situation in the early sessions. Don't worry about it; as you feel more at ease, your body will relax into the natural responses of the orgasm.

The relaxation-breathing and spoon-breathing exercises can be put to practical use here to reduce uptightness and nervousness in the case of difficulty. This technique of sharing while taking responsibility for your own pleasure can be integrated with many other kinds of mutually stimulating variations. Increase your options: use masturbation as a quick warm-up to intercourse; stimulate your clitoris or penis during intercourse; stimulate your breasts during masturbation with partner, etc.

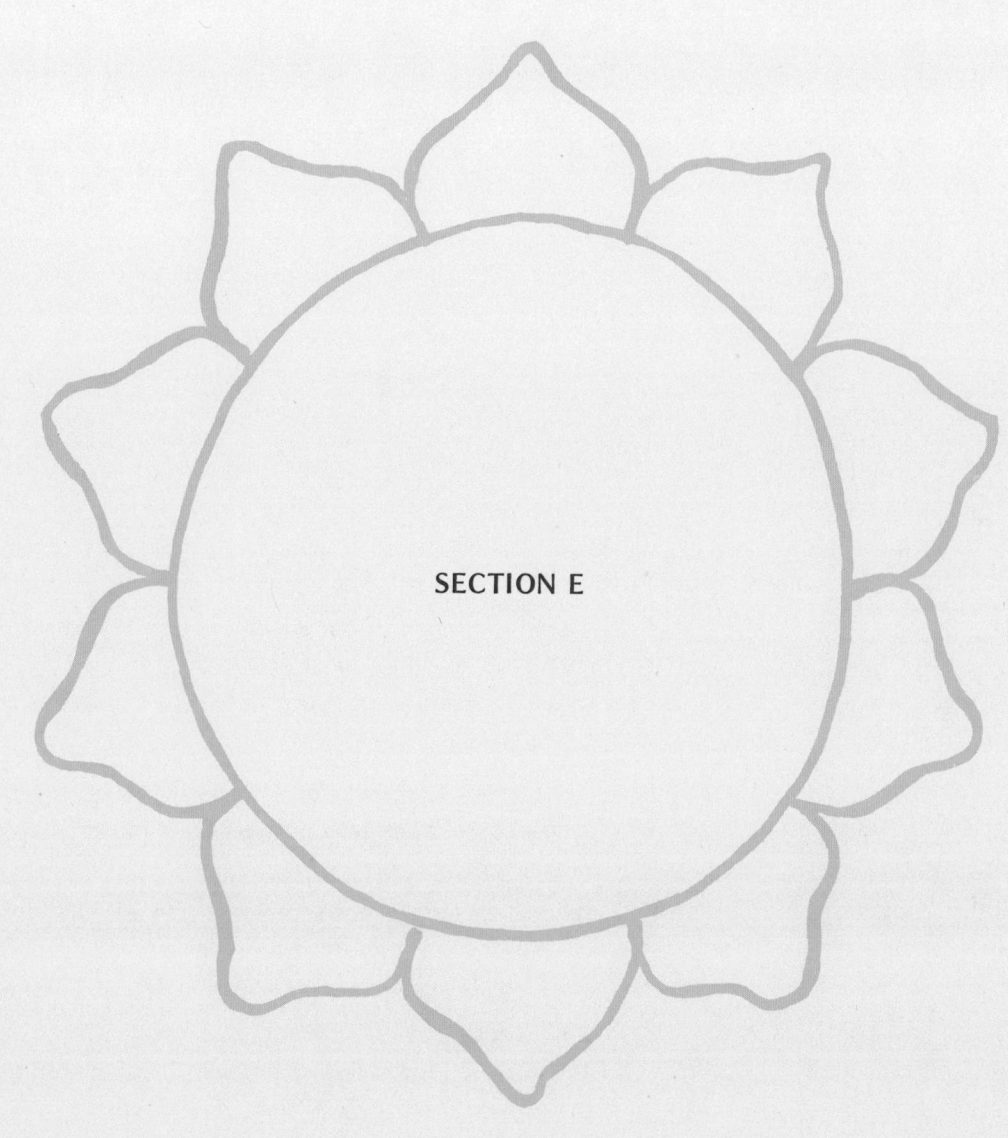

SECTION E

DISABILITY

THE SEXUAL MINORITIES

One of the most oppressive results of sexual ignorance in our society has been the myth that persons who are disabled, either physically, mentally, or emotionally, are not sexual. This includes persons whose bodies are "unattractive," who do not fit our media image of "beautiful" or "smart." There are approximately forty million persons in our country today who are classified in the group of totally or partially disabled. Paraplegics, quadraplegics, cerebral palsied, schizophrenic, blind, mentally retarded, heart patients, diabetics, amputees, etc., are all victims of community and professional ignorance and infantilization.

   The fact is that people feel sexual regardless of their disabilities and want and need accurate sex information and positive attitudes to develop their natural abilities and potentials. A degree of sexual satisfaction is possible in most cases, and the disabled usually report that sexual satisfaction is very important to them as it is to all of us.

   The first large group of disabled persons to express this sexual need happened to be the spinal cord injured, para- and quadraplegics. Dr. Theodore Cole of the University of Minnesota began counseling some of his patients in a rehabilitation center in the late nineteen sixties. Out of that early experience came a growing awareness of the kinds of information and methods required to help disabled people learn about their sexual possibilities and develop their sexual potential.

   The needs of this group for special attention and support, although specifically aimed at the spinal cord injured, are applicable to any of the other persons labeled disabled as well as to able-bodied persons.

1. There is a strong need for accurate information about the physiology of sex for the disabled.
2. Lack of accurate sex information is a definite deterrent to a person's sexual development.
3. Touch and intimacy are important to the overall health of all persons.
4. People need to learn how to communicate their needs and desires to their partners.
5. Personal exploration and experimentation are vital to the growth of sexual relationships for the disabled.
6. The disabled must develop responsibility for their sexual self image and for their sexual activity.
7. The disabled need to learn what their sexual options are. (Just what can they do?)
8. Persons who need options must be taught the techniques of oral and manual sexual stimulation.
9. Throughout the learning process, professional support is needed to encourage experimentation and skills.
10. For some people, a psychological or mental sexual experience needs to be explored and developed.
11. Cooperation from attendants and hospital personnel in securing fantasy materials and privacy for sexual activities is necessary.

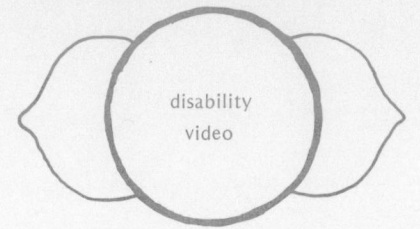

This is only a partial listing of the areas which should be considered and explored with persons who are disabled. Of necessity, this is a very brief consideration of a very important and complex field. For those of you who would like to delve further into this subject, we recommend the following:

Rabin, Dr. Barry J. *The Sensuous Wheeler, Sexual Adjustment for the Spinal Cord Injured.* San Francisco: Multi Media Resource Center, 1975 (in press). Paper. This book is written both for those who are disabled and for those who would be of service to them (nurses, doctors, friends, etc.). Although fairly technical, it contains good basic information of a sex positive nature. An extensive bibliography of the field is included.

VIDEO—WEEK 4.

"TOUCHING." The man in this film is a quadraplegic; he has a sixth cervical vertebra injury. There is some residual sensory feeling around the coronal ridge of the penis, near the anus, and on the back and edge of hands. The woman is able-bodied. The couple has changed their sexual focus from a purely genital focus to the oral and manual aspects. They take their time, not rushing. The woman has several orgasms. The man has occasional "reflex" erections not evident in the film.

"THE SQUEEZE TECHNIQUE." This film demonstrates a method of helping men control their ejaculation. The structured approach can be spontaneous and fun.

"EROGENIST." The film shows continual body contact during massage. The man focuses on awareness of woman's response. Pay particular attention to sex flush, muscle tension build-up, breast enlargement, and the high degree of intimacy.

"GIVE TO GET." The woman massages the man over his whole body with a particularly sexually arousing focus. Emphasizes non-demand pleasuring of penis, with a variety of strokes. They have intercourse on a waterbed, making use of the motion of the water to aid thrusting.

The two films, "EROGENIST" and "GIVE TO GET," show a variety of different pleasuring techniques for the man and the woman.

HOW TO CONTINUE THIS COURSE

First of all look at your progress:

1. What new things have you learned?

2. What has changed?

3. How do you feel about your initial contract now?

4. What was your reaction to the video films?

5. What else do you want to change?

6. What tools (options, attitudes, behavior) do you have to continue sexual growth?

7. See your sexual self now. Describe:

8. If you have a partner, describe any changes that have occurred during this course.

Now look at your future:

1. Describe the sexual self you desire in the future.

2. What must you do to reach that future self?

3. How will you do these things? When? With whom?

At home exercises to concentrate on:

1. In general masturbation gives us our baseline knowledge of what is effective stimulation. It is most likely to produce orgasm and is a reliable learning experience. Therefore it is important to continue the masturbation exercises you find helpful on a regular basis.

2. Kegel exercises are helpful throughout the rest of our lives to keep our genitals in a healthy condition. Do something to remind yourself to do them.

3. Learning how to touch more pleasurably is also an on-going process. You may want to re-read the sections on Sensate Focus and Massage.

4. Learning to feel close, loving, trusting with our partners can continue forever. Give yourself a chance to explore all the exercises listed with partners.

5. Continuing to unlearn sexual negativity can be done by re-reading the informational reading in Section C.

6. Check out the bibliographies listed in each section if you're interested in a particular subject.

AT HOME EXERCISES FOR ENRICHMENT

	Section E Page No.
30. Masturbation with Sounds	120
31. Enrichment through Fantasy	121
32. Enrichment through Oral Sex	122

Repeat Exercises

Go back over the exercises you have learned and repeat those you especially enjoyed. Focus on exercises that will help you grow in awareness and confidence (Kegels, Yes and No, etc.).

AT HOME EXERCISE 30—MASTURBATION WITH SOUNDS

Making sounds while you masturbate can enhance your involvement, your turn-on level, and your sense of the experience. Many people learned to masturbate very quietly so that no one would find out what they were doing. Making noise while masturbating is a natural way of expressing our feelings.

If you already make sounds, listen to them. If you rarely or never make sounds while masturbating (or lovemaking) take a few minutes to consider what the constraints might be. Are you worried that someone will hear you? You never thought about it? It's not "nice"? It's not feminine? It's not masculine?

After you have explored your present pattern of making (or not making) sounds, begin to experiment with some new alternatives:

1. Exaggerate the sounds you make.
2. Use new words, growls, moans, whispers, panting, screaming, laughing.
3. Make new sounds, loud or soft.
4. Time the rhythm of your sounds to go along with your stroking or body movements.
5. Explore non-vocal sounds, such as bed squeaking, fingers squishing, sheets rustling, air whooshing in and out of your vagina.

All these patterns and combinations can change with your mood and the particular situation. For example, how do you feel about sharing these sounds with your partner?

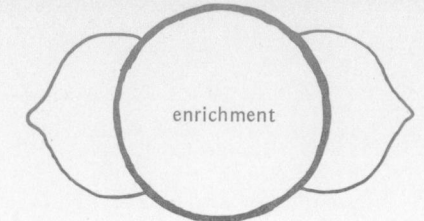

AT HOME EXERCISE 31 — ENRICHMENT THROUGH FANTASY

These are suggestions. Play with those that appeal to you.

1. Spend an hour allowing your favorite sexual images to appear on the screen of your mind.
2. Develop one of these images in great detail, conjuring up the environment, colors, smells, tastes, touches, sounds and textures.
3. Develop a fantasy that you can act on alone.
4. Tell your fantasy to at least one other person.
5. Agree to spend some specific period of time acting on a fantasy with a partner.
6. Build a mutual fantasy using elements of your fantasy and someone else's.
7. Be a different sexual character for 24 hours.
8. Express yourself as a person of the opposite gender for 24 hours.
9. Read at least one piece of erotica or pornography.
10. *Draw* your cunt/cock.
11. Fantasize with a person of the same gender.
12. Buy an object to improve your sexual image.
13. Make one positive comment about your sexuality to three people.
14. Have a sexual experience before dinner.
15. Write an ad for a lover.
16. Interview a consenting partner for the job of your lover, master, slave, wife, husband.
17. Wear a costume to bed.
18. Fantasize about a past sexual experience while masturbating.
19. Masturbate while talking over the telephone to a consenting friend.
20. Develop a detailed fantasy that incorporates your personal sexual needs and your sexual politics.

E

AT HOME EXERCISE 32—ENRICHMENT THROUGH ORAL SEX

Many people practice and enjoy oral sex.

Many people find oral stimulation an effective route to orgasm.

Many people feel that oral sex provides its own unique kind of pleasure.

If you do not yet feel comfortable with oral sex, begin by having a talk with your partner about your feelings and limits. Begin by taking a bath or shower together, exploring each other with your eyes while you explore yourselves with your hands, then vice versa. As you dry yourselves, smell and taste each other. One person should now become the *receiver* and one the *giver*. The giver then explores the partner's body orally, seeking to pleasure the partner and get feedback from her/him, but mainly to pleasure the giver with whatever s/he feels comfortable doing to the receiver.

The giver may: lick
                suck
                stroke
                hold
                mouth
                tongue
                nibble   the receiver . . . .

The receiver may provide feedback with sounds and body movements.

Some things to do when giving oral sex to a man:

1. Hold the penis gently but firmly in your mouth.
2. Caress the penis with one or both hands.
3. Caress the penis with breasts or other parts of the body.
4. Lick the entire penis like an ice cream cone.
5. Lick the underside of the penis from the base to the tip.
6. Gently squeeze the testicles.
7. Rotate the penis on its base.
8. Run your tongue under the coronal ridge.
9. Nip gently at the testicles and shaft.
10. Hold the tip of the penis in your mouth.
11. Use both hands as well as your mouth.

Make up some more items for this list.

Keeping a quantity of saliva in your mouth will help the penis taste more familiar to you and supply a natural lubricant.

Some people like the taste and consistency of pre-ejaculate and semen. Others dislike one or both. (The same person's fluids may taste different from time to time.) Both these fluids are safe for consumption. Some people think that increasing water intake and eliminating acid beverages (like coffee) will improve the flavor of semen; others say drink lots of orange juice. Whatever experiments you try will probably be interesting in this regard.

If you do not wish to swallow semen, see if you can find another use for it, like rubbing it all over your body, or on your partner.

Some men feel badly if their partners don't like their semen. But rejection of the taste and viscosity of semen

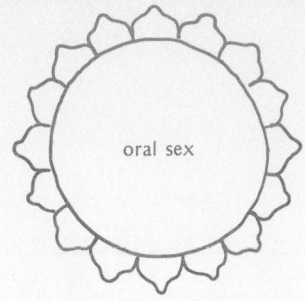

is not the same thing as rejecting the lover as a person. Talk it over with your partner; taste your own come again. You might not like it either.

Some things to do when giving oral sex to a woman:

1. Rub the mons gently.
2. Lick from the vagina to the top of the clitoris.
3. Make a circle around the clitoris with the tip of the tongue.
4. Stroke each inner lip slowly.
5. Gently tug on the hair on the outer lips.
6. Carefully separate each part of the genitals with your tongue.
7. Do the same with your fingers.
8. Lightly nip the tip (or glans) of the clitoris.
9. Put a finger or two into the vagina slowly.
10. Put a finger into the anus; go slowly.
11. Use your hands or your tongue to penetrate the vagina.
12. Use the tip of your tongue, the flat part, the edge.

Invent some new stroke and savor it.

After your experience share with each other about how you felt.

Now let's concentrate on the receiver's pleasure. The receiver instructs the giver in the kinds of stimulation s/he wants. The giver practices the strokes, pressures, and rhythms, and controls amounts of lubrication that the receiver asks for.

Several of these sessions will enable you to know what you and your partner(s) like. These preferences may change, so continue to give each other feedback. The feedback may be varied also; sometimes verbal, with sounds or body movements, or all of these, etc.

When you have learned to focus while both giving and receiving, try giving and receiving simultaneously.

E

APPENDIX

LUBRICANTS

Body secretions, vaginal lubrication: self-made, safe anywhere.

Vegetable (salad) oil: right out of the kitchen.

Hand and Body Lotion (Elizabeth Arden): unscented for genitals; two scents for general body use.

Natural Honey (Revlon): good for general body use and genitals.

Lotion 2000 (Bonne Bell)

Lubriderm

Vaseline Intensive Care Lotion: seems okay for genital use even though Vaseline is not.

Swedish Formula Hand Lotion (Max Factor)

Oil of Olay

Albolene Cream (Norcliff Labs): a popular massage medium; can cause irritation if used on female genitals.

Lotion for Hand and Skin (Neutrogena): okay for genitals.

General guidelines: Any oil or lotion is okay for general body use subject to individual differences like allergies. Lotions for genitals should be unscented, contain no alcohol and not alter natural vaginal acidity. Often the only way to test a lotion is to try it. The lotion may be used sparingly on the inner lips before trying it on the clitoris. If it proves acceptable on the outer genitals, it can be tested inside the vagina. Lotion testing can be great fun. The expense can be reduced by sharing small "tester" portions within a group.

GENITAL HYGIENE

I. Women

Natural odors from the genitalia are not bad or offensive in a healthy woman. Secretions from inside the vagina usually have a sweetish odor that changes as the secretions move to the outside and are exposed to the air. The advertising media has tried to reinforce the message that "down there" is dirty and needs deodorizing. Disinfectant douches and genital deodorants are potentially harmful and generally troublesome.

Basic Guidelines to Follow

1. Plain warm water will remove all the secretions. Clean in the folds of the lips and around the clitoris and hood once or twice a day or as you feel necessary.

2. Do not use deodorant soaps or anti-bacterial detergents. They remove natural oils and bacteria that are necessary for keeping the vagina and outer genitals healthy, and can cause dryness and cracking. Vaginal infections can occur with much greater frequency when the natural balance is upset. If you use soap at all use a pure soap like Ivory and use it only on the hairy parts and outer lips. Beware of inexpensive bubble bath products which may irritate the genitals.

3. If you are concerned about odor it may help to keep your pubic hair trimmed short.

appendix

4. After a bowel movement, be sure to wipe from front to back, and not vice versa. Bacteria from the anus do not belong near the opening of the vagina or urethra. Wash the anal area whenever convenient instead of merely wiping with toilet paper.

5. Douching too often can sometimes upset the natural balance of the inside of the vagina. A general rule of thumb is to douche each month after your period to remove old cells, and to use only the solutions listed below. If you feel like you want to douche more often you can, but stick to the safe solutions.

   Generally safe solutions
   1. Two quarts water to 4 tablespoons white distilled vinegar.
   2. One quart water to 1 tablespoon white distilled vinegar plus 2 tablespoons *plain* yogurt (acidophilus culture).

6. If you notice an odor that seems bad to you it may be an indication of an infection and it would be a good idea to check it out at your local clinic or with your doctor.

7. If you find you frequently have vaginal irritations or infections, try switching to cotton underpants. Cotton absorbs moisture better than some of the new synthetic and nylon pants and allows more air to flow around your genitals.

II. Men

1. Heavy use of deodorant soaps and anti-bacterial soaps can remove natural oils and cause dry skin on the penis, scrotum and perineum. Use pure soap like Ivory on your genitals.

2. Wash around the genital area, paying special attention to the crevices (and under the foreskin if not circumcised) at least once a day.

3. After a bowel movement wash the anal area whenever convenient instead of merely wiping with toilet paper.

SEXUAL CONCERNS

Many people have sexual experiences that result in a feeling of failure. These experiences may happen only occasionally and therefore fall into the natural ebb and flow of all of our sexual life experiences. If sexual experiences frequently feel like failures, they can be a source of anxiety and concern. The most well known of these concerns are listed in the chart below.

Concern	Technical Definition	Comments
Women:		
1. No orgasm	Pre-orgasmic (hasn't happened yet)	Check for: —effective stimulation —time spent on pleasure of self and masturbation

Concern	Technical Definition	Comments
2. Dissatisfaction with reliability of orgasm	Situational or secondary orgasmic concern	Check for: —adequate and effective stimulation —positions that allow access to clitoris for stimulation —letting partner know what might or does turn you on
3. Pain during sex	Dyspareunia	Check for: —effective stimulation —need for added lubrication —exam for vaginal infection —exam for general physical condition of pelvic organs and abdomen
4. Vaginal muscle tightening to make vaginal penetration very difficult or impossible	Vaginismus	Check for: —feeling of tightness, pain or spasm at vaginal opening —exam for vaginal infection —exam for general physical condition of pelvic organs

Men:

Concern	Technical Definition	Comments
1. Difficulty beginning or maintaining an erection	Erectile failure or impotence	Check for: —adequate and effective stimulation —fatigue and stress —being in the mood to have sex —general physical health —use of alcohol or other drugs known to reduce erection potential —letting partner know what turns you on
2. Ejaculation very quickly or before you want to	Premature ejaculation	Check for: —time spent on pleasuring self and masturbation —taking time to get more satisfaction for self —previously learning to have sex or masturbate quickly

ABOUT THE AUTHORS

TONI AYRES is a public health nurse with a B.S. degree in nursing, who has been a sex educator, coordinator, and sex therapist at the U.C. Medical Center Human Sexuality Program for the last three years and recently received a faculty appointment to the U.C. School of Nursing in Family Health Care. Ms. Ayres has also been a faculty member of the National Sex Forum and consultant for media program development since 1971. She is co-director and co-founder of San Francisco Sex Information. Her specialty is in the design of sex education process and materials and women's sexuality groups.

PHYLLIS LYON is a co-founder and co-director of the National Sex Forum as well as being an author, lecturer, and active feminist. She is a founder of the Daughters of Bilitis, an international Lesbian organization which began in San Francisco in 1955, and of the Council on Religion and the Homosexual. Her current interests revolve around women's concerns, female sexuality, the Lesbian, and social change. With her partner of 22 years, Del Martin, she has written the books *Lesbian/Woman* and *Lesbian Love and Liberation*, as well as numerous articles. She is also a member of the board of Genesis Church and Ecumenical Center and San Francisco Women's Centers.

TED McILVENNA is a co-founder and co-director of the National Sex Forum and one of the leading figures in the field of sex education both in this country and abroad. A Methodist minister (he has a M.Div. degree), he brought his talent for creation and design of new methods of radically humanizing social problems to the sex field. Currently he is President of the Board of Genesis Church and Ecumenical Center. He is the editor of the *YES Book of Sex* series as well as author of several of the books in the series, and has written and lectured extensively in the field of human sexuality. One of his current concerns is in the field of First Amendment rights and he has appeared in many court cases involved in freedom of speech issues.

FRANK R. MYERS, a media coordinator, has been with the National Sex Forum since 1971, designing and developing media materials and programs using the SAR process. His background includes a B.S. in psychology and several years of experience in research and teaching in nursery and primary school education. Graduate studies include programmed learning techniques, computer systems and design, and experimental psychology. Other skills include expertise in massage and body work, environmental design and coordinating of the SARguide project.

MARGO RILA is the coordinator of San Francisco Sex Information, a community telephone service which provides sex information and referrals. She has a B.A. degree in Sociology and a background in social work, encounter group work, and sex education. She is also on the Associate staff of the University of California Medical Center Human Sexuality Program and is a consultant to the National Sex Forum.

MAGGI RUBENSTEIN is a psychiatric nurse who gained extensive experience during six years at San Francisco's Center for Special Problems. She has been a core staff member of U.C. Medical Center's Human Sexuality Program in the Sex Advisory and Counseling Unit since its inception. She is co-founder and co-director of San Francisco Sex Information, a free community phone service, and has been a faculty member of the National Sex Forum and consultant to the media process for three years. She is currently working on an M.A. in psychology, with emphasis on bisexuality and androgyny. She is a native San Franciscan, 44 years old, has two teenage children, Sarah and David, and is an active feminist. Her life keeps getting better. She has extensive experience in psychodrama and is an accredited associate director. She plans to continue to develop psychodrama as an effective technique in sex education and counseling.

CAROLYN SMITH has dedicated her professional career to studying and researching body awareness and self knowledge techniques as a way to overcome social, sexual and other personal concerns. She has an extensive background in counseling and her expertise includes bio-feedback, relaxation techniques, breathing awareness, fantasy development and positive reinforcement behavior modification. She is a pioneer in the emergence of the field of sex education and sex therapy and has developed many new innovative techniques for self-help for men and women in her work at the U.C. Human Sexuality Program. She has also designed and consulted on programs for single men's sexuality groups.

LAIRD SUTTON began his work as media director of the National Sex Forum in 1968, surveying the whole field of human sexual behavior including sexual patterns, media needs, and recording information. Since 1969 he has created over forty sex documentary films and tapes to bring together a basic body of material that can be used in sex education, sex therapy, sexual enrichment, and teaching methodology. Future plans include exploration of the range of possibilities for use of the video media in dealing with sexual concerns and sexual enrichment. He also plans to further his country lifestyle and ecological concerns. In addition to the above, Mr. Sutton holds the following degrees: B.A., B.D., S.T.M., and has been a Methodist minister for the last 16 years.

Concern	Technical Definition	Comments
3. No ejaculation	Inability to ejaculate	Check for: —time spent on pleasuring self and variety of masturbation techniques —effective and adequate stimulation —going past the level of sensitivity if sex is prolonged

Since the sexual response cycle is the result of effective stimulation (what turns us on), there may be environmental causes for some of our concerns. These might be socio-cultural constraints, overriding emotional states such as depression, health and drugs, and our feelings toward our partners. These may be non-productive stimuli in the sexual response cycle. Only you can get to know what turns you on. Only you can let your partner know what you like. If you have taken the time to follow the at home exercises, put energy in communicating to your partner and feel you are still stuck with a concern, you may want to seek the guidance of a reliable sex counselor in your community. If you feel you are making progress, give yourself credit and congratulations.

ADDITIONAL RESOURCES

The National Sex Forum can provide information as to where authorized Personal Sexual Enrichment/Education (PSE/E) programs are being given around the country. The Forum cannot provide the names of individual sex therapists or counselors in various areas, nor can we answer by mail specific questions about sexuality. Specific sexual questions can be answered by calling San Francisco Sex Information in San Francisco. Trained volunteers staff SFSI's phones Monday through Friday from 3 to 9 p.m. Simple factual answers are given to direct questions. The telephone number is 415/665-7300.

All of the books listed in the SARguide can be obtained by mail from Multi Media Resource Center. A bookstore catalog listing many of the available books is available from MMRC. Please enclose 25 cents to cover handling and mailing.

Multi Media Resource Center has also created a fully annotated Bibliography listing some 300 non-fiction books, pamphlets and comic books on human sexuality. Cost is $3.00.

In addition, MMRC publishes and distributes the *YES Book of Sex* series designed by the National Sex Forum. The series currently includes five titles: "You Can Last Longer" by Herbert E. Vandervoort, M.D., and Ted McIlvenna, M.Div.; "Getting in Touch/Self Sexuality for Women" by Toni Ayres, Maggi Rubenstein and Carolyn Smith; "Lesbian Love and Liberation" by Del Martin and Phyllis Lyon; "Gay Men Speak" by Ronald D. Lee in collaboration with Frank Melleno and Robert Mullis; and "When You Don't Make It" by Ted McIlvenna, M.Div. All the books are illustrated.

Information on the National Sex Forum's films and on the video cassette package for use in the PSE/E program can be obtained from Multi Media Resource Center.

ADDRESSES

NATIONAL SEX FORUM
540 Powell Street
San Francisco CA 94108
Phone: 415/989-6176

MULTI MEDIA RESOURCE CENTER
540 Powell Street
San Francisco CA 94108
Phone: 415/421-5035